Chip -
This Book will @
Bless you So

M000200101

Hearing
God:

The Ultimate Blessing

Seven Secrets to Hearing God

Hearing GOD:

The Ultimate Blessing

Seven Secrets to Hearing God

Raymond Ho

Jacket design by Koechel Peterson & Associates, Minneapolis, Minnesota

Destiny Image® Publishers, Inc.
P.O. Box 310
Shippensburg, PA 17257-0310

"Speaking to the Purposes of God for This Generation
and for the Generations to Come"

ISBN 0-7684-2073-3
Library of Congress Catalog Card Number 2002-141111

For Worldwide Distribution
Printed in the U.S.A.

This book and all other Destiny Image, Revival Press, MercyPlace,
Fresh Bread, Destiny Image Fiction, and Treasure House books
are available at Christian bookstores and distributors worldwide.

For a U.S. bookstore nearest you, call **1-800-722-6774**.
For more information on foreign distributors, call **717-532-3040**.
Or reach us on the Internet:
www.destinyimage.com

DEDICATION

This book is dedicated to the loving memory of my late father
Kenny

and
to the four most important women in my life
My mother Ruby,

My sister Maria,

My wife, Tere,

My daughter, Leslie.

Endorsements

"*Hearing God* touched both my heart and soul with a warm spirit that drew me closer to God. Its practical wisdom, penetrating insights and pointed anecdotes will help any seeker learn how to enter into the presence of God and hear His voice for divine guidance. *Hearing God* will change your life!"

Al Kasha
Two-time Academy Award-winning Songwriter,
Producer, and Author

"Raymond Ho has provided a glimpse into a subject about which so many are interested. From having worked with Raymond Ho, I can unequivocally say that he is a man after God's heart and his insights should help each person desiring greater intimacy with God."

Tommy Barnett
Phoenix First Assembly of God

"With this extraordinarily candid debut, author, former chief executive, and filmmaker Raymond Ho takes his place beside those in a long eminent tradition of spiritual autobiography.

Hearing God is bold, witty and incisive. Where Samuel Beckett posited a world "Waiting for God"—a world of cynicism, despair and desperate hope—Ho has asserted cohesive optimism, multiplying "the good word" into a remarkably succinct and intimate declaration. This one man's long and arduous journey, courageously unveiled, bespeaks an accessible, compassionate God who transcends denomination, separatism, gender, even species, embracing all that is good, joyous, and loving. Ho lays it out clearly: How he believes God—the spirit, whatever you want to call the force that animates the world—communicates directly with people in today's miasma of a world. It is fresh, penetrating and passionate, with a rare intensity both warm and unflinching. This is a book that will be read and talked about for years because it dares to be practical and is wise without saying so."

Dr. Michael Tobias
Ecologist, Author, Filmmaker

"Raymond Ho's *Hearing God* is superbly written—fresh and honest, objective and incredibly concise. It is designed to speak to the masses, not just to the cloistered church. It should become a classic!"

Dr. Larry Ward
Former White House "Ambassador to the Hungry World"

CONTENTS

An Excerpt From
My Spiritual Journal

Dear child:

Do not listen to other voices; listen to ME, the voice of GOD.

Everyone would tell you their version of reality, but I will tell you the naked truth. Their reality is based on their subjective experience of truth; it is only a partial truth. What I reveal is the truth, but your finite mind and limited concentration can absorb only small glimpses of truth, which become your reality.

No one has ever fully comprehended the truth. Why? Because I AM TRUTH.

Because I AM INFINITE and man is finite, no man has ever mastered THE TRUTH.

No man has fully understood GOD.

I am not only a GOD OF TRUTH, I am also a GOD OF LOVE, I am a GOD OF MERCY, I am a GOD OF CREATION, I am the GOD OF EVERYTHING. I AM ALL THERE IS!

So never mistake a student as the MASTER. A student never calls attention to the student, but only points the way to the MASTER. People mistake the student as the Master because they can see the student, but they cannot see the Master. They can hear the student but cannot hear the Master.

I want you to write a book that will point the way to the Master. I want you to teach the students to seek the Master themselves, not the master teacher. Why? Because I AM THE MASTER. I am the original. A copy of the original is not as perfect as the original. A copy of a copy is not as good as the copy.

The reason people mistake the copy for the original is because they have not taken the time to discover the essence of the original. It is much easier to accept others' packaged truth, mistaking their limited perception of truth as THE TRUTH and their finite perception of God as THE GOD.

Therefore, point the way to ME, but do not let your finger block their vision of ME.

Do not let them focus on you, but on ME. As they seek ME, they will find ME. They will find GOD and discover THE SOURCE OF TRUTH.

This will set them free from the errors of partial truths. Two half-truths do not add up to a whole truth.

I ALONE AM TRUTH. IF ANYONE WANTS TO KNOW THE TRUTH, THEY MUST COME AFTER ME.

INTRODUCTION

IF GOD TALKS TO PEOPLE, DON'T YOU WANT TO HEAR HIM?

> If you lack wisdom, what do you lack?
> If you lack wisdom, what do you have?
>
> (Midrash)

If God talks to people, don't you want to hear Him?

Well, He does talk! And He is trying to talk *to* you and *with* you.

Hearing God: The Ultimate Blessing shows you seven secrets to hearing God. It reveals timeless spiritual truths on how to enter into His presence and how to tune in and listen to His communication.

We all have the capacity to hear from God. We all have the ability to know His will. We can all receive His divine guidance.

Are you facing confusion, chaos, or crisis in your life? Are you carrying the burden of loss? Are you coping with broken relationships? Are you dealing with the pain of financial reversal? Are you searching for meaning and purpose for your life? Are you tired of the drudgery of lifeless religion? Are you striving for a deeper spiritual life? Are you trying to change but don't know how?

God has the answers to these perplexing questions of life, and if you ask Him, He will help you discover the answers. He will talk to you by His Spirit.

This book will lead you to the path where you will discover how to plug in, turn on, tune in, listen, and hear the voice of God. It will enable you to detect His many forms of communication and how to respond effectively. It will teach you the process of discerning the voice of God and distinguishing it from other voices in order to avoid fatal errors.

The Purpose of This Book

This book is intended to inspire you to seek and find the source of divine wisdom for your life and the place of intimate communication with Him. Wisdom is knowledge of God and knowledge from God. It will provide you with inspiration, direction, and strength to face whatever trials and tribulations you encounter in your world. It will lead you to the place where you discover that you are not alone on this journey.

There you will discover the secrets of the Kingdom. You will forever stop striving and never arriving. You will stop grasping and start giving. You will stop chasing blessings and begin to be a blessing. You will stop hoping for a miracle and start being a miracle.

My inspiration for this book came from a divine encounter with God at 3:00 a.m. on Friday, April 17, 1992. That day I heard the voice of God unmistakably for the first time. It saved my marriage and changed my life forever!

Prior to that, I had only heard *of* God but never heard *from* God. When you hear about God, you get secondhand knowledge from others who experienced God. When you hear God, you receive wisdom, knowledge, and understanding directly from Him. The first is an intellectual exercise of the head; the second is a spiritual experience of the heart.

After my encounter with God, I knew the difference between knowing about God and knowing God. I finally discovered that God is not only *real*, but that He also desires to *talk* to people!

And, if we have the faith to obey what He says, we step into the world of the miraculous and receive our ultimate blessing.

Since that day, I have been pursuing God with a vengeance to hear from Him again.

I did, and His communication was captured faithfully in thirteen spiritual journals during a ten-year period.

Then one day while in the midst of listening, He told me that He hadn't given me these revelations just for my use. If I didn't share them, I would be spiritually "constipated," and the revelations would stop.

So, reluctantly, I read some passages to a few friends and colleagues. To my surprise, they were so touched by the words that some cried, and others prayed as if they had heard from God directly.

God then placed a greater burden on me to share what I had learned more widely. That is why I wrote this book.

Therefore, I dedicate this book to God with all my love—and to everyone who is seeking Him.

Let me state up front that this is not another one of those "God told me" books, in which the author claims to have all the answers to the challenges of our world because he has a special line to God. Frankly, I am skeptical about such claims. I don't want to give God a bad name, and I certainly don't need a spiritual malpractice suit filed against me when I arrive at the gates of Heaven.

No, I don't have all the answers to the mysteries of the universe, or to the problems in your world. But I can show you from experience some steps of how to get through to the One who does. I can help you penetrate the mystical veil of religiosity and the metaphysical world of spirituality. I can show you the narrow path to God's holy presence that I discovered, so you, too, can find the answers to life's perplexing questions.

There is no one single perfect formula for hearing God that will work for everyone. God is infinite, and He has numerous ways of communicating. He created each of us distinct and unique, and His communication with each of us is equally special and personal, based on our relationship with Him.

Neither is God a celestial hot line where you can deposit a few prayers and get through to Him for a spiritual chitchat session. God has a sovereign plan, and He speaks with a purpose. He communicates His will to those who are ready to listen, follow, and obey. When God speaks, it requires a response on your part.

JOURNEY OF A GOD SEEKER

This book is also about my incredible journey as a God seeker. Hopefully my story will help you identify in a personal way with some of the obstacles a pilgrim will encounter in his or her journey. I'll be sharing some adventurous stories about my amazing encounters with God. They produced results that can be described only as miraculous!

Like you, I am a God seeker, a fellow pilgrim on a spiritual journey. I have sought after God for many years now, and I still seek Him earnestly daily. I will always be a seeker, until my spirit is permanently reunited with Him for eternity.

God is timeless. He is the same yesterday, today, and forever.[1] True spiritual laws and principles are never new; they are based on timeless truths. This book reveals seven such principles in a simple, practical, and entertaining way. The purpose is to help you learn and apply them in your own life, whatever your spiritual orientation.

IF YOU SEEK GOD, YOU WILL FIND HIM

If you read this book and commit to seeking God with all your heart, you will find Him! He will show you how to walk with Him, talk with Him, and hear from Him. And He will never fail to give you the divine guidance, comfort, conviction, and correction that will bring you to your knees and bring you to your senses.

Throughout your journey, you will hear and experience the love of God as you learn to commune with Him. I encourage you to immediately capture what He reveals to you in your own spiritual journal. Then you will discover for yourself that hearing God is the ultimate blessing!

As a final note, I wrote this book in a relaxed and conversational style so you won't get a headache from reading it. Life has enough headaches of its own. I purposely kept the writing simple without being simplistic. But don't be fooled; God is anything but simple! Yet, neither is He so mystical that He is beyond the reach of your understanding.

We humans are created of God, made in His image.[2] We have the capacity to understand God, if we learn how to listen. Then we can hear His wisdom, follow His directions, obey His instructions, and live an abundant life beyond our "self."

When you get to know God, you will hear Him. When you hear God, you will want to obey Him. And when you obey Him, you will receive the ultimate blessing.

God is truth, and His word is truthful. When you act on what He says, you will experience the power of truth in action. It will set you free—free from illusions and delusions; free from errors in thinking and mistakes in action; free from doubts and fear; and free to live and love.

If you live in fear,
You will fear to live.

If you live in love,
You will love to live.

If you believe in love,
You will love to believe.

The meaning of life is love.
The meaning of love is to give life.

(Anonymous)

Endnotes

1. See Hebrews 13:8.
2. See Genesis 1:27.

CHAPTER 1

THE FIRST TIME I HEARD HIS VOICE

> God does not cease to speak, but the noise of the creatures without, and of our passions within, confines us and prevents our hearing. We must lend an attentive ear, for his voice is soft and still, and is only heard by those who hear nothing else!
>
> (Francois Fenelon)

If you want to hear God...

SECRET #1: Believe there is a God, then plug in, turn on, tune in, and start listening.

If you want to hear God, you first have to believe there is a God.

Let's begin with a story.

"Do you believe in God?" the priest asked his dentist.

"Hell no! I am an atheist," he answered with a laugh.

"Do you believe in hell?" the priest pressed on.

"Absolutely not! It's all a figment of the imagination," said the dentist.

"An atheist is someone who knows there is no God, right? Then let me ask you another question. Of everything there is to know in dentistry, how much do you know?" asked the priest.

"Quite a lot," said the dentist. "Do you see all those certificates on the wall? That was my formal education, but I have also practiced professionally for thirty years!"

"Of everything there is to know in the whole world, how much do you know...twenty-five percent? Ten percent? One percent?" the priest continued his line of questioning.

"Let's say ten percent," the dentist replied.

"Then isn't it possible that God might exist in the other ninety percent that you don't know?" said the priest.

"Well, you've got me there. I am not an atheist, then; I am technically an agnostic...I don't 'know' if God exists," the dentist said. "But I still don't 'believe' there is a God."

Most people don't have that much of a problem believing that there is a God out there, as long as "it" is defined as a cosmic intelligence that gives order to the universe. What most people get hung up about is what kind of God is this? Is it a He, She, or It? What is God like?

GOD HAS ALWAYS TALKED TO PEOPLE

Throughout the history of civilization, various cultures have described God in many ways with different names. The Jewish people call God ELOHIM, which is Hebrew for "Supreme Being," as well as YHWH (Jehovah), which expresses God's essence. For Christians, God is a God of the Trinity with the Father, Son, and Holy Spirit. ALLAH is the name that the Muslims use, which to them signifies "The One True God."

Throughout the ages, people attempted to capture the nature and presence of God that they experienced. They developed concepts that still influence many people today. The perceptions of God that many in society hold today often come from the subjective experiences of what these men and women have "heard" from God in the past.

The divine communications came to them in the forms of visions, dreams, messages, and revelations. They captured and wrote down these communications in words. Later, many of these writings became the bases for various holy books found in religions across the world.

The Torah of the Jews is a collection of Jehovah's revelations and directives to the prophet Moses. The Koran, as the Muslims believe, was Allah's messages to the prophet Muhammad through the angel Gabriel. The Bible of the Christians is a compilation of God's communications through forty authors, in three different languages, over thousands of years.

In time, these subjective, personal, and sometimes dramatic revelations were accepted and adopted as objective truths. They became the foundations for establishing the spiritual truths of these religions. The followers of each believe that their book alone contains the authentic, accurate, authoritative, and infallible Word of God.

Although distinct differences exist in their interpretations and concepts of God, they all agree on one point: God talks to people! Otherwise, how could the prophets have argued the authenticity of their revelations? The very strength and authenticity of their words is based upon divine communication.

WHY AND HOW GOD COMMUNICATES

Since God is eternal, He is not dead. And if God is alive, then He is still speaking.

The question is: Is anyone listening?

Now, first you must realize that God is love and He loves us. He speaks out of His loving nature and desire to be with us. Love is His basis and reason for communing with us.

Love must always have an object, and with God it is no different. *We* are the objects of God's love. We are His highest form of creation. We are made in His image, with the ability to understand, receive, and reciprocate His love.

Like any good father or mother, God loves His children. Unlike some parents, He loves us with a perfect love that is unconditional. He longs to relate and commune with us, for He created us to have a loving relationship with Him. And love requires communication.

Now, for communication to take place, there must be a sender and a receiver—a transmitter and a decoder. Effective communication requires both a speaker and a listener.

When God communicates, He is the sender and we are the receivers. His Spirit is the transmitter and our spirits are the decoders. Meaningful communication is always a two-way exchange of messages between two parties.

Prayer is our communication to God. Meditation is our listening to God. Revelation is God's communication to us.

God is the source of all wisdom, knowledge, and understanding. He is the source of all truth. He is the source of everything!

He is omnipotent (all powerful), He is omniscient (all knowing), and He is omnipresent (ever present). He is eternal, immortal, infallible, immanent, transcendent, and sovereign. Now, these are theological concepts that tend to isolate mankind from God. When we *hear* God, He is no longer an abstract being to us, but a living reality. It is His words that draw us into a circle of relationship. He steps out of theological imagery to become our *Friend*.

That is why we need to hear from Him. That is why hearing God is the ultimate blessing!

WHY CAN'T WE HEAR GOD?

Now, God is everywhere; He can communicate anywhere, at any time, and in any way He chooses.

God reaches out to communicate to us all the time and in many ways. We are not aware of it because we are not paying any attention. We don't know how to discern His various forms of communication.

It is as if God is always broadcasting, but our tuner is not plugged in. If it is plugged in, then it is not turned on. If it is turned on, then it is not tuned in. If it is tuned in, then we are not listening. Even if we are listening, we are still not *hearing* Him.

Listening and hearing are two different things. Most of the time when our radio is on, we don't know what is playing. We are too busy doing something else so we don't hear the song, let alone the lyrics. It is just background music when we are not listening with concentration.

When we focus our attention, we can really hear the song and appreciate the beauty of the lyrics. And if we listen intently, we can even feel the emotions of the songwriter and soar on the melody of the song if we sing along.

Like the radio station that is always broadcasting its signals, God is always communicating with us in different ways, hoping that we will plug in, turn on, tune in, listen, and hear Him. God loves you, and He wants an intimate relationship with you. He is trying to reach you, if you would only learn how to hear what He is saying and communicate back to Him.

For forty years of my life, I ignored God's many attempts to reach me. My tuner was not plugged in because no one had explained to me that God communicates with ordinary people. I thought He only spoke to His chosen few—to prophets, saints, and those who are "holy."

Since I was not on this short list, I never turned on my tuner. The few times I tried when facing difficult situations, I got static noise instead, and no one showed me how to fine-tune my listening to get a clearer signal.

Since I never heard from God, I thought that either there was something wrong with me or there was something wrong with those people who said things like, "God told me this and the Lord told me that."

I thought they had to be deluded to think they had a direct line to God. I saw them as self-righteous, religious bigots who set themselves above everyone else like me, who never heard from God.

THE DAY I HEARD GOD'S VOICE

Everything changed on Friday, April 17, 1992, at precisely 3:00 a.m. I was desperately seeking God with all my heart and soul. I was facing mounting pressures at work, and my second marriage was on the rocks even though we were a newly married couple. I was like a lost ship looking for a lighthouse in the dark of a stormy night.

I had hit rock bottom. I was at the end of myself and was on my knees seeking God. Suddenly, out of nowhere, a still, small voice started speaking gently. I was stunned! I knew it was not my thoughts speaking. It was unmistakably an external voice and not my conscious mind.

It said, *"Love your wife, Tere, unconditionally as I have loved you. I have shown you mercy; I have given you grace; I have forgiven your sins so that you may do the same for your brothers and sisters. Begin with your wife, Tere. I have sent her to purify you. Through her, you will learn love and forgiveness. If you love and forgive, you shall have peace. And whenever you stumble, I will be at your side to pick you up again."*

In an instant, that voice convicted, corrected, and comforted me all at the same time. An unexplainable sense of peace swept over my whole being. I was so dazed by the experience that I frantically looked around for anything on which to write down what I had heard.

Later that morning, I shared the experience with my wife and read to her what I had heard. I followed up by reading her a letter of apology I had composed after hearing the voice, and I sought her forgiveness. Tears started streaming down her face as if a dam in her heart had just cracked.

I didn't know what to do or what to say, so I got out a notepad in an attempt to work out our differences with the Ben Franklin method. I drew a line down the middle of the page to analyze the pros and cons on both sides. I was determined to get to the bottom of our problems and resolve them, since all our marriage counseling sessions had failed.

To my utter amazement, I could not identify a single problem to write down at that moment. Not one! How could this be? Something must really be wrong. After all, we had been fighting over so many issues: money, who was being controlling, the family members, and then the big one—the prenuptial agreement!

How was it possible that I couldn't identify a single problem now? Had I gone insane from not having slept all night? Finally, an uncontrollable laughter exploded out of me as if I had just won the lottery.

A sense of bliss engulfed me in that instant. I knew beyond the shadow of a doubt that some kind of miracle had happened, even though I couldn't understand it at the time.

By being in the presence of God the night before, my mind had been transformed by what I "heard." Before an infinitely big God, my seemingly insurmountable problems shrunk in size. They became so small and petty that I couldn't find them the next day.

Now, I would be misleading you if I told you that our marriage was totally healed that night. It wasn't. But that experience was certainly the first evidence of a progressive healing process that saved our marriage. It also started my intensive ten-year journey of searching for the secrets of the spiritual kingdom that eventually changed my life.

That search has led to many revelations, miracles, and a chain of events that changed my world.

But, what really happened that night?

PLUG IN, TURN ON, TUNE IN, AND LISTEN

First, I believed in the possibility that God was real and that He could help me if I asked. I plugged in my "radio" and turned it on out of sheer desperation. I asked for God's help after all the psychologists, psychiatrists, and marriage counselors had failed. Later it seemed so absurd to me that I turned to God as my last resort when I could have sought Him first. Isn't it strange that God is often the last line of our search?

Second, I was actively tuning in to hear God. I was asking, seeking, and knocking on Heaven's door.

I was finally facing a mountain too big for me and I had no way around it. I was between a rock and a hard place. The woman I loved more than anything in the world was also the one who was in psychological combat with me daily. I had one and only one purpose: to find God and ask Him how to get out of this misery. I had to hear from Him, even if it took all night to find the right frequency.

Third, I was completely focused and determined; I was not going to be distracted by anybody or anything. I had left my bedroom and gone to the little room where I do my reading and meditation.

At 3:00 a.m., everything is totally quiet and you can hear a pin drop. No wonder I could hear God's still, small voice when He finally spoke.

Fourth, when God communicated, I believed and did not doubt. I respected His wisdom and captured His direction on paper. I wrote it down, read it several times, and meditated on it until I understood what God really wanted me to do.

Finally, I demonstrated faith by obeying His instructions immediately the following morning. This was timely and reverent obedience; it was faith in action. It was only when I acted on what God said that I saw the power of truth. It was my first encounter with the supernatural and my first experience with the miraculous.

That day, God gave me the revelation that hearing Him is the ultimate blessing. *When I heard from God, I was "blessed" by His word of truth. The true state of blessedness is when we can experience love, peace, joy, and hope independent of our outward circumstances.*

Now I understand why the Scriptures say, "Man does not live on bread alone, but on every word that comes from the mouth of God."[1]

Endnote

1. Matthew 4:4.

CHAPTER 2

LOOKING FOR GOD
IN ALL THE WRONG PLACES

How silent are God's voices. How few men are strong enough to be able to endure the silence. For in silence God is speaking to the inner ear.

The door between God and one's own self must be kept ever open. The knob to be turned is on our side.

(S.D. Gordon)

If you want to hear God…

SECRET #2: Look for God at the bottom of your valley of despair, for He is waiting for you. Just give up, give in, let go, and let God be God.

If you are looking for God, don't look for Him at the mountaintop.

> He is not there. Your ego is there…taking up all the space.
>
> If you want to find God, look for Him at the bottom of the valley.
>
> He is waiting for you…to come to Him.
>
> At the pinnacle, there is not enough room for two gods.
>
> God is big! He won't fight with you.
>
> There is more room for Him in the valley…of your despair.

For most of my life, I did not know that I was looking for God in all the wrong places. I climbed many mountains hoping to find what I was looking for, but I discovered that beyond every mountain is always a higher mountain. But, subconsciously, I was really running from God because of my hidden sin, shame, and guilt.

I was not doing His will because I was too busy doing *my* will.

A PILGRIM'S JOURNEY

I want to tell you my personal journey of how I found God, and the most unusual places where I found Him.

> I didn't find God at the mountaintop.
>
> I didn't find Him at the synagogue.
>
> I didn't find Him at church.
>
> I found God on my knees at the bottom of my valley of despair.
>
> You will find Him, too, when you've stopped trying to be God.
>
> You will find Him when you give in, give up, let go, and let God be God.

I had never been the religious type. I had no concept of God or the spiritual world. Frankly, I thought religion was a real bore!

I grew up as a Catholic in Hong Kong, with my mom taking us to church every Sunday. The only thing I liked about church was that we got to go out to lunch afterwards as a family. Church was a weekly activity that had no meaning to me because I had no personal relationship with God.

I was baptized as a baby and had my religious training as a child. I memorized the Lord's Prayer and the Hail Mary. I studied my catechism and received Holy Communion, but they were meaningless rituals to me because God was only a concept. He was not real. It was like someone telling you about a far-off galaxy that you know you will never experience.

So for many years, I had no relationship with God, even though later I realized that on many occasions He had been trying to reach me as a father would his long-lost son. I was too busy with the pursuit of the good life. I never took time to listen to God. In fact, I never knew that you could hear God, let alone talk with Him.

I was so driven and self-centered that I never made time for anyone else in my life either, except those who could help me further my goals. I had no time for God because I was trying so hard to be the god of my own life. I wanted to succeed on my own. I wanted to be the captain of my ship and the master of my destiny. Besides, I was taught that God helped those who helped themselves.

Since I did not know God, I was receptive to all religious thinking. I did think that there must be a God, otherwise why would every religion teach about some sort of ultimate being? But, I had never experienced Him. I had heard of God, but I had never heard from God. He was too profound, too big, too good, and too distant for me to reach.

While at boarding school in England, I was exposed to the Quaker tradition. By the late 1960's, I was a student at the University of Wisconsin in Madison, where freedom was the religion. We worshiped our freedom; pot and sex were our gods. We cherished our freedom of expression and exercised our right to challenge the existing authorities.

After graduate school at Syracuse, I converted to Judaism in order to marry my Jewish wife. It was not a big issue to me; my father, who was steeped in Confucianism, had converted to Catholicism to marry my mother. Besides, I presumed that all religions pointed to the same God like rivers run to the ocean. So I accepted the Jewish faith and became part of a Jewish family for the next sixteen years. I even had a rabbi as brother-in-law. He was a little skeptical because, in spite of my conversion, the glass didn't break the first time I stepped on it as part of the Jewish tradition during my wedding ceremony to his sister.

During the next decade, I secretly adopted another religion: It was called "Me, Myself, and I."

The idealism of the 60's was soon replaced by the "me generation" of the 80's, to be followed by the ultra-materialism of the 90's.

I found out one thing: The Chinese and the Jews share a lot in common beyond their love of Chinese food and reverence for education. It's money, money, money! So, I pursued my career goals with a burning passion and climbed the ladder of success with a rare determination to satisfy the expectations of both my Chinese parents and my Jewish in-laws.

When I was growing up, my father used to say, "Beyond every mountain there is a higher mountain." It was his way of saying, "Keep striving, and never let it get to your head."

That's how I became addicted to the challenge of the impossible, just like some people are addicted to drugs and alcohol.

YOUNG AND RESTLESS

By my early thirties, I had become the head of a five-station PBS television network in Arkansas, succeeding a seventy-two-year-old state senator. For me, it was no big deal because no one was dying to go to Arkansas. The people of Arkansas have a saying, "Thank God for Mississippi!" because then Arkansas doesn't always have to rank last in the polls.

This network in Arkansas was described by some in the industry as being "beyond repair." Apart from the low level of funding, the powers that be had a habit of blacking out parts of Masterpiece Theater programs when they thought those parts were too racy for the South.

At thirty-two, I had reached my first mountaintop. I became the youngest person running a public television network, working for the youngest governor in the history of the United States. His name was Bill Clinton.

I was so thrilled when Governor Clinton called to welcome me. I had never talked to a governor before. My ego was swelling with his every word...until he requested that I find a job at the network for a former worker in his gubernatorial election campaign.

This was evidently a routine procedure with my predecessor, but I was so naïve about politics. I protested with my chairman and refused Clinton's request. Out of courtesy I decided to interview this gentleman. In the end, I hired him so I could learn the ways of the South. That was my first lesson in politics.

Even though I was not a "good ol' boy" from the South, I soon developed a love affair with the people of Arkansas. The network became a source of pride for the state, winning more than thirty national awards for excellence. *Esquire* featured me in their "Man At His Best" issue and honored me as "one of the men and women under forty changing the nation." This was the beginning of my ego trip up the next mountain.

Some legislators speculated that I was another Bill Clinton, using Arkansas as a stepping stone for greater things. I was discreet when other networks began recruiting me. I made them promise to keep everything strictly confidential and to never contact my board members without permission.

One day, Hillary Clinton called. By then, I knew she was no ordinary woman. She was a powerhouse! What in the world would she want from me? Since I had blown my last encounter with her husband, I was in quite a panic.

Mrs. Clinton was gracious with her opening compliments, but within seconds she cut to the chase. "Raymond, you're a real asset to Arkansas. The people of this state love you, so don't leave us now. We can achieve a lot together under this administration. I can help take care of your problems with the legislature...."

My ego was really enjoying the conversation until I came to my senses. *How does she know that I am being wooed by other networks?*

Mrs. Clinton continued as if she had read my mind. "The superintendent of education in Maryland and I serve on a national board together. He asked me, 'Truthfully, is Ho as good as he says he is?' And I answered, 'Yes, and more!' "

CLIMB EVERY MOUNTAIN

That took me to the next mountaintop in Maryland. At thirty-five, I became president and CEO of Maryland Public Television, one of the largest PBS state networks and a major national producer for the nation.

Now my ego was really starting to grow. I thought I could do just about anything. I soon learned that the ego is the biggest stumbling block to our spiritual journey.

At that time, our program "Wall Street Week" was the highest-rated program on money and finance in the country. As the new CEO, I extended an invitation to its host, Louis Rukeyser, to meet me in my office.

A message came back from his secretary: "Mr. Rukeyser said that if Mr. Ho wants to meet him, Mr. Ho will have to come to Mr. Rukeyser's office."

Beyond every mountain there is indeed a higher mountain. Dad forgot to tell me that on top of every mountain there are many giant egos fighting to stand at the same pinnacle. The taller the mountain, the bigger the egos and the rougher the battles.

On my way to see Louis, I ran into a small Asian man who bowed his head and greeted me in Japanese. I had no idea who he was or what he was saying. Later that night, I turned on PBS and there he was on "Wall Street Week" talking with Louis in perfect English. He was Akio Morita, the legendary founder and chairman of SONY.

Every week I would run into movers and shakers of the financial industry. They were giants like Federal Reserve Chairman Alan Greenspan and Fidelity Investments' superstar Peter Lynch...all guests of Louis. I met many CEOs, stars, musicians, politicians, and moguls over the years from all our shows.

THE EGO TRIP

During my first month on the job, our network won an Emmy for one of its programs. Shockingly, we beat out all the major networks—CBS, NBC, and ABC. Even though the program was produced before I arrived, it didn't stop me from taking all the glory.

Anyone can look good in a tuxedo next to an Emmy. That was the beginning of my love affair with awards.

I have always been a quick learner, so I started to develop my own programs and stars to make my mark on our industry. In time, we won dozens of national and international awards, including another Emmy with Julia Child.

Soon we were producing hundreds of hours of programs for PBS and broadcasters worldwide. Once we did a star-studded "Great Performances" program with Judy Collins, Andy Williams, Tony Bennett, Bernadette Peters, Glenn Close, and others...but I didn't have time to meet them. I was too busy surveying the next mountain, preparing for more adventures ahead.

Soon I was not content to be a co-star with an Emmy. I wanted to be a star in my own right.

I appeared on television and radio networks, did interviews with newspapers and magazines, and held press conferences in Washington, London, and Tokyo to promote my vision for global programs with global partners for a global era.

I had my thirty seconds of fame, too. I was featured on the front covers of a few magazines, as well as the *Washington Post*.

I was on NBC's "Today" show and in *USA Today*, *Chicago Tribune*, the *New York Times*, and many media outlets. Overnight, I was becoming a celebrity of sorts—in my own imagination.

I enjoyed the perks that came with the territory: exotic trips to places like Cannes and Rio; use of the governor's yacht and stadium box; and invitations to great parties, balls, and VIP events. I attended receptions at the White House with President Ronald Reagan and later President Bill Clinton.

The most memorable event was a Washington luncheon with Queen Elizabeth and the Prince of Wales. Even senators, moguls, and celebrities like Ted Turner and Jane Fonda had to wait in line, just like I did, for over an hour for the Queen's arrival.

Yes, indeed, beyond every mountain there is a higher mountain. And beyond every ego there is always a bigger ego.

SOMETHING ELUSIVE WAS ALWAYS MISSING

Over the years, I enjoyed six-figure salaries, made seven-figure deals, and managed nine-figure budgets. I was a millionaire and lost a million, too, in one year. I entertained my ego with the usual toys for men—Rolexes, Mercedes, a house with a pool, a house with a view, and a house on the water.

I had a great job, a successful career, a responsible wife, and a beautiful daughter. I had everything...except peace and contentment. Something elusive was always missing, but I never knew what.

After feasting my eyes on those tall and tan, young and topless girls on the beach of Ipanema during a business trip, my ego presented the answer to my discontentment. "My dear Raymond, you need more love in your life. You will have peace and contentment when you find true love. Get yourself a new wife who really appreciates you. Then you will have everything!"

I was shocked when my wife agreed to an amicable divorce. We had moved six times while I was climbing those mountains and it had taken a toll on our relationship. I had been so obsessed with my work that I didn't know she had felt neglected for years. A sixteen-year marriage ended just like trading in a car.

The following week, I met the most beautiful woman in the world. I was getting made up for a television appearance, and my makeup artist was a gorgeous Colombian named Tere. She was my dream come true. It was love at first sight...fireworks were going off...and songs were gushing out of my heart like a fountain. I was falling in love all over again and it was bliss.

We were swept away in ecstasy and flew off to the beaches of Mexico and Bermuda, and then to London and the French Riviera. I was happy. I was content. I had found true love! I had found heaven on earth! I wrote and recorded "I'll Give You All" and sang "You Are My World" at our wedding ceremony.

Little did I know that war was about to break out immediately after our honeymoon. Her engagement ring and our wedding rings soon turned into "suffer-rings." How could something so wonderful change so quickly?

The woman I loved became my worst enemy. My "dream come true" had become my worst nightmare. My heaven on earth turned into a living hell!

THE EGO DECEIVED AND BETRAYED ME

What happened? The ego I had fed all those years deceived me. It was my best friend, but it betrayed me. I didn't know what went wrong, and I didn't know what to do. For the first time in my life, I felt like a complete failure. Like Napoleon, I had met my Waterloo. I descended into the bottom of my valley of despair...where I found God waiting for me.

That night when I heard the voice of God, I discovered that I could not fully trust my "self" anymore. The ego can cause so much static that you can get a bad transmission and be easily deceived. Everything I had believed as truth for years shattered in a moment like a bottle that just hit the ground.

What happened to all my powerful worldly paradigms that had given me so much "success" over the years?

I had been lured into the trap that says, "I am the master of my own destiny. I can create my own future. There is no reality except what I create. There is no truth except what I choose to believe."

The naked truth was that my world was falling apart, and I had no idea what had happened or what to do.

Little did I know that, in the spiritual world, my life had to crumble before it could come together. Falling apart and coming together are the same; before the new can be birthed, the old must die; before we can be filled, we must be emptied.

That was the night when the reign of my ego ended. I crucified it before God. It was also the beginning of my spiritual journey; God had brought me to my knees and brought me to my senses. It was the start of giving in and giving up, of letting go and letting God be God. It was the first step in a journey of a thousand miles in my search to find God, seek His help, and hear His words.

For every problem, God has a solution.

Our first step to hearing God is to humble our "self" before Him, confess that we have a problem, and admit that we need His help.

When we finally raise the white flag on the mountain of our ego, God is ready to help. God can't visit us unless we invite Him. He can't feed us unless we are hungry for truth. He can't fill us until we are emptied of self. He can't talk to us unless we are ready to listen.

The French philosopher Pascal said that man was created with a huge inner vacuum that could be filled only with God. The great end of this spiritual journey is where nothing in my will is contrary to His will.

...Those souls who tend towards God merely by the intellect, even though they should enjoy a somewhat spiritual contemplation, yet [they] can never enter into intimate union, if they do not quit that path and enter this of the inward touch, where the whole working is in the will.

—Madame Guyon

CHAPTER 3

IS YOUR TUNER STILL WORKING?

> ——→ The voice is a spiritual voice, unattended by
> material sounds or the pain and torment of them, but
> rather with majesty, power, might, delight, and glory
> ...an infinite interior sound which endows the soul
> with power and might.
>
> **(St. John of the Cross)** ●——

If you want to hear God...

SECRET #3: Let your ego be subdued and nourish your spirit, for it is your spiritual tuner.

CAN MAN HEAR GOD?

Can man really hear God? Can we mortals hear from the
voice of the Immortal? The answer is *yes*!

We are made in the image of our Creator. *God created us with
the capacity to commune with Him.*

He gave us a mind, spirit, and body. The spirit is the eternal and immortal part of us; it is our spiritual tuner that is capable of hearing and communicating with God.

God is spirit.[1] In the spirit world, there are no physical barriers like time, space, or matter. The spirit world is not confined by the limits of our human measurements like mathematics, physics, or chemistry. The spirit operates in a dimension that transcends and confounds us.

In the invisible spiritual world, thought is the highest form of energy, so if God thinks it, it can happen…it will happen…it has already happened. Whatever God thinks and speaks into words, happens, because His word has creative power and does not return to Him void. *Hallelujah!*

We can't grasp it or understand it because it is not visible to the human eye, at least not yet. Why? Because we operate in a limited dimension, and even our definition of reality is inadequate. Our concept of time is strictly linear and our interpretation of reality entirely restricted by what we can perceive with our senses.

So when God speaks to us, what He says is already a "done deal" in the spirit world. For us in the physical world of matter, however, it has the *potential* to happen, if our spirits believe in His word and have the faith to act upon it. "In the beginning was the Word"[2]—and the Word is the physical expression of God's thoughts. God's thoughts as expressed in His words have the power to create and the energy to move mountains. When God spoke, "Let there be light,"[3] the creative force of His word brought forth light out of total darkness.

HOW FAITH CAN MOVE MOUNTAINS

You've heard the saying, "Faith will move mountains!" When our spirits receive a transmission from God—and we believe in our minds and act with our bodies—we ignite a spiritual energy that can move mountains in the physical world. How?

First, God transmits His message to our spirits. The spirit transmits to the mind, and the mind commands the body to act. Together our spirits, minds, and bodies transmit the message to others through our voices, words, and other forms of expression. Now a spiritual chain reaction has started, initiated by the thoughts and words of God.

Spirit controls matter, and whatever is stronger moves what is weaker. When we have faith to believe in God's word, we have a "knowingness" founded on His truth. This gives us the spiritual power to enlighten, and the physical energy to inspire others to action. Then we attract the necessary provisions to move mountains, one shovel or one bulldozer at a time.

Just as love needs an object for its affections, so faith needs a "word" for its actions. When faith is "pregnant," it always conceives actions because the way to release faith is to act. So something that began as a pure thought, reflecting the will of God in the spiritual world, can now move matter in our physical world. What a miracle! *Praise God!*

When God purposes something, He transmits His thoughts to us through communication. He can do this in many ways through thoughts, words, or pictures. He can communicate any way He chooses, using any medium of transmission. He can use people, passages in a book, scenes from a movie, scenes from nature, dreams, visions, and the spoken word.

THE FIRST MOUNTAIN I MOVED

Let me bring this down to earth with some real-life examples. After my encounter with God, I left my career in public broadcasting to serve the needy. I became a vice president at Food for the Hungry, an international relief and development organization that served the poorest of the poor around the world.

One day several videotapes mysteriously arrived at my office unsolicited. Out of curiosity, I looked at them. They contained horrific scenes of torture and persecution of the people of Sudan.

Christians were being hatcheted to pieces because of their religious beliefs. It made me sick in my spirit.

I knew that God was using those scenes in the tapes to convict my spirit to act. I was new to the world of relief work, and I thought helplessly, *What can one person do?* There was no money in the budget, and even if I could raise the money, there was no way to get the relief supplies to the victims because the fighting was taking place in a "no-fly zone." These were the mountains blocking my spiritual vision.

Then God used an Asian police officer-turned-pastor to teach me the principle of how faith moves mountains. As the Spirit of God spoke to this man, he risked his own life and traveled to the front line of the fighting in Sudan. He was so moved by the horror and suffering of the people there that he had to do something, so he adopted a Sudanese baby and brought him home to the United States.

When the man returned, he spoke to his congregation and introduced his new Sudanese baby. He showed the horrific video footage he had captured and transmitted passionately to them through his spirit, voice, and pictures. His message penetrated deeply through the spirit of everyone in his congregation.

When the word began to spread, people responded with an unprecedented outpouring of contributions that enabled this pastor to buy a used plane to deliver relief supplies. At great risk to his life, he led missions into the "no-fly zone" with volunteers from his church and brought relief to the victims.

That was mountain-moving faith! This man found a way when there seemed to be no way. He accomplished what I thought was impossible, because he had the faith to believe and obey what God had transmitted to him through His Spirit.

Later, I was watching the news during the time Hurricane Mitch hit Central America, and God convicted me again. When I saw those helpless victims waving for help from the rooftops, surrounded by torrents of flooding water, I knew I had to do something. But what can one person do?

It was early in the disaster, and our advertising age
thought it would be prudent to wait. To be blunt, they didn't think
the body counts were high enough to justify a major campaign
yet; it would be too risky. My rational mind agreed, but my spirit did not.

God was transmitting to me, *"Don't just stand there; do
something! Remember what I taught you about faith that moves
mountains?"*

A MILLION-DOLLAR MIRACLE

Since I could not convince the advertising agency or my
boss, I asked God, "We don't have any money in the budget, what
can I do?"

He directed me to sow a financial seed for a financial harvest and
invite all the managers to do likewise, to show our commitment.

At a staff meeting, I said, "This morning I was praying and God
told me to write a hundred-dollar check to help the victims of
Mitch. He invites you to join me and show that we are committed
and united. I know most of you already contribute to many chari-
ties. But how can we ask God or the donors to help if we aren't willing to set an example? God said that if we would unite and sow
into this harvest, He would multiply our seeds a thousandfold."

The "transmission" convicted their spirits, and they dropped
checks and cash into a collection. The $100 turned into $1000
instantly. Then a miracle started in the mail-processing room that
turned into $100,000.

The ladies in the processing room were not aware of what we
were doing. They were praying for a million-dollar month in their
collections. The amount was up to $900,000, and time was run-
ning out. It would take a $100,000 miracle to make the million.
That day, an unknown man contributed $100,000 to support the
victims of Mitch after hearing the news. (He might have been an
angel for all I know!)

This was enough to convince our advertising agency to start
a major radio and direct-mail campaign. That first hundred-dollar
seed soon became a multi-million-dollar harvest in cash and

.multiplied my tiny seed not just a thousand and times! God is faithful.

TO MULTIPLY YOUR MIRACLE, KEEP
.NG

As .ansmission went out to the Hispanic community, contributions started to pour in when a Hispanic radio station got involved. Twenty-five, forty-foot-long trucks loaded with food, medicines, and emergency supplies came. It overwhelmed us and became our new mountain. We had to use a military air base to sort out these mountains of supplies before we could ship them. Little old ladies, living below the poverty level, gave their last enchilada.

To broaden the transmission, we approached Home Depot, and they bought a full-page ad in *USA Today*. They asked their customers to donate old tools through their stores so our teams could rebuild homes and communities devastated by Mitch. The campaign swept across the nation and surpassed our wildest imaginations. Yet, it all started by hearing a word from God.

By the time we faced the next international crisis in Kosovo, we had internalized the truth of this spiritual principle and were able to raise several millions of dollars to help the victims without any fanfare. What I once thought was a miracle was, in fact, a basic spiritual truth I had not understood before. And it all began with hearing a transmission from God, then believing and acting upon it with faith.

ARE YOUR SPIRIT, MIND, AND BODY
IN HEALTHY BALANCE?

God is spirit, and God is holy. He speaks to our spirits through His Holy Spirit. Our spirits are the innermost part of us that is created by God to receive spiritual transmissions. It is our god-self, the higher self, the "real" self—the part of us that is eternal, immortal, and indestructible. Our spirits cannot die because the spirit is not physical and it is not confined by time, space, or matter.

God created our spirits to have communion with Him. Therefore, our spirits yearn to commune with God even though our minds and bodies might be too busy to notice or cooperate. *Our spirits long to hear God. The spirit needs wisdom, knowledge, and understanding from Him like the body needs food, water, and rest.*

If we want to hear God, we have to make sure our spirits, minds, and bodies are in healthy balance. We exercise our minds during every waking hour and we feed our bodies several times a day, but how often do we nourish our spirits?

When our spirits are healthy and functioning properly, we can send and receive clear transmissions without interference. When the communication is working, we can hear the Holy Spirit reveal truth, which is the natural, healthy diet for our spirits.

God wants to communicate with us so we can have the direction we need to live a good life. He wants us to live an abundant life that is bigger than our "self." But, there is a problem.

To obey God's words, our spirits must take control of the mind and body. The ego deceives the mind into thinking that the ego is the "real" self and not the spirit. It poses itself as the best friend of the self and proves its loyalty by constantly gratifying self. The ego feeds the appetites of the body and satisfies the passions of the flesh.

I remember the time when my mind, body, and spirit were totally out of balance. I fed my mind with self-help books like *Seeds of Greatness*, *The 7 Habits of Highly Effective People*, and *Unlimited Power*, while my brain was pickled in alcohol and my spirit was chained up by my ego.

In the television business, we always had a good reason to drink—it was a great day, it was a bad day, we closed a deal, we lost a deal. Every year in Cannes—the world's largest television market—we would start the morning with champagne and orange juice, then float through the day with back-to-back meetings—over drinks, of course. Everyone had a "fabulous" project that was "about" to go into production and they just needed start-up funding. Believe me, the only way to maintain your sanity was to be on cloud nine and laugh at the whole scene.

With the books I was cramming into my brain and the drinks I was pouring down my throat, I was feeding my mind and poisoning my body at the same time. When I prayed, nothing ever happened. I never heard from God. My brain was filled with soulish thoughts, but my body was constantly exhausted, and my spirit was shriveled up like a prune. My spirit, mind, and body were at war with one another.

THE EGO DECEIVES AND SEDUCES

The ego not only deceives the self into seeking constant and instant gratification, but it also seduces the self into developing a self-centered and self-serving lifestyle. The ego presents an unrealistically high estimation of itself and an inaccurate low estimation of others. It feeds itself with a steady diet of pride, making itself larger than it is. The center letter to the word *pride* is "I"—it is all about me, mine, and myself.

Let me tell you a story about how the ego deceives.

While I was at Maryland Public Television, every year during contract renewal time, I would dread the prospect of going through another battle with Louis Rukeyser, the host of "Wall Street Week." Louis was the most popular and influential network television personality in financial reporting at that time. He had a special gift of making the often-dry subject of finance fascinating. The viewers loved his wit.

In show business, when you are hot, you are hot! At contract renewal time, or any time for that matter, you can demand the sky and work your way down to earth. I had no problem with the fact that Louis made six times more than I did for one day's work per week. I wasn't jealous of his five-figure speaking fee or the tremendous royalties from his books. After all, Louis was a real star, and "Wall Street Week" was our most profitable show.

My ego just couldn't take all the theatricals during contract renewal time. I felt like a cornered animal and wanted to fight back. Since Louis had hinted about offers from other networks, I decided to make plans to diversify the funding for the series. If he left, we would need some other stable avenues of income. I mocked up a "Wall Street Week" newsletter and showed it to him. He was livid when he saw that his face had been reversed. The graphic artist had mistakenly reversed the negative, but no one would have noticed the difference. The concept died a quick death.

A few months later, I discovered to my amazement a newsletter called "Louis Rukeyser's Wall Street" in my in-box. And it was selling like hotcakes! It became the highest grossing newsletter of all time, raking in more than ten million dollars the first year.

I was furious! The newsletter was my idea, and I had been up front about it. I even offered Louis a percentage. This newsletter came without warning, and the network received absolutely nothing from it.

Our dispute soon blew up publicly in the *Washington Post*. Even Bob Dole, the Republican Senate leader at the time, weighed in on the Senate floor of Congress. Among other things, he criticized PBS for having such inept leadership that we "gave away the store." Ouch! That was painful to my ego.

Now Louis' contract was up for renewal, and we were at the proverbial Mexican standoff. Louis refused to renew his contract. Now, this contract contained a provision that either party could get out in thirty days. Every year, that clause hung over my head like a guillotine during those sleepless nights.

I knew that we owned the show and could always replace the host; no one is irreplaceable. Our attorney thought we had a case against the newsletter on infringement of our name. But it was highly risky because the sponsors might pull out if Louis left. What should I do?

After many long agonizing nights, I asked God for direction. He told me to forget the lawyers. They were shooting threatening letters back and forth like fiery arrows, and the negotiations were going nowhere.

God said, *"Go and apologize to Louis at his home and ask him for his forgiveness."*

THE THREE MOST POWERFUL SENTENCES

My ego couldn't believe what I had heard.

I fought back. "But, God, I'm not the one who's done anything wrong, so why should *I* apologize? What do I apologize about?"

My spirit told me to obey.

With great apprehension, I went to see Louis at his Connecticut home. When he opened the door, I extended my hand but he did not reach out with his. The tension in the air was so thick I could hardly breathe.

I thought, *This is going to be one long, tough visit.*

I obeyed God's word, though, and recited what I was told. "Louis, I am very sorry, and I ask your forgiveness."

Nothing happened. There was no miracle. The problem was that my heart was not in it; I did not expect it to work.

In faith, I repeated myself, "I am very sorry about my comments in the papers. It was totally taken out of context, and I know it has hurt you."

After a long pause, I swallowed hard, summoned up all my inner strength, and said, "Louis, I love you. I am sorry. Will you forgive me?"

There was a long pause…silence was ringing in my ears until I could hardly stand it anymore.

Finally, Louis opened his mouth and replied slowly, "I understand how the press can be…I accept your apology."

We spent the next two hours breaking down the walls separating us. He told wonderful stories of the early days of the show. It turned out that the thirty-days clause was put there not by

Louis, but by our executive producer. She wanted the option to replace Louis quickly in case he bombed.

After that, we called off the lawyers. Everything was resolved by a simple, one-page letter. That day, I realized again that hearing God is the ultimate blessing.

Through that experience, God taught me several important lessons that I would never forget for the rest of my life.

> *Lesson #1:* The three most powerful sentences in the world are these: I love you. I am sorry. Will you forgive me?
>
> *Lesson #2:* Do not judge.

My ego had deceived me into judging Louis. I had built up resentment and anger in my heart against him for various reasons. When the newsletter incident came, my anger overflowed into the press and created a war. However, I didn't know all the facts, let alone the truth. I had pre-judged him, which is what prejudice is.

That day, I learned that the ego is the archenemy of the spirit. It is always at war against the spirit that longs to hear God. It is constantly trying to dominate and conquer the spirit and *edge God out*. That's why it is E-G-O.

The spirit is eternal; it has a spiritual sensitivity or awareness that comes from God. The ego, on the other hand, is shortsighted and blind; it lives only in the here and now. It knows nothing of eternity.

The ego sees no further than the boundary of the self; it sees self as separate from others. The world is something to be mastered so as to strengthen the position of its world.

The spirit, however, recognizes that it is part of a larger whole. It recognizes that God created everyone and everything and that He loves *all* of His creation. We are all brothers and sisters of the same human family.

Therefore, when our spirits are in communion and union with God's Holy Spirit, our egos die and our spirits come alive. We trade in our pride for humility as He gives us the self-assurance that eliminates the need to prove to others the worth of who we are or the rightness of what we do. Our desires are turned from ourselves to others as we seek to love, give, and forgive others.

HOW TO NOURISH OUR SPIRITS

When we seek God for His direction, we are tuning in to His Holy Spirit—the source of truth, wisdom, knowledge, and understanding. He is a wonderful counselor and a fountain of loving communication.

If we want to hear God without static, we must learn to nourish our spirits. We do that by setting aside quiet time to feed our spirits with truth. What we put into our spirits will determine our spirits' health and affect the clarity of our hearing. What we put into our spirits determines what comes out. What are we putting in?

Our lives are powerfully affected by our thoughts, and what we think depends on the influences we permit to enter into our lives—people, books, music, television, movies, etc.

After twenty-four years in television, it still amazes me that the average American family has its TV set on for seven hours and twenty minutes each day. We have a saying in the TV business, "You can never underestimate the lowest common denominator."

Why are we surprised to see airplane hijackings and terrorist bombings in the news? Why are we shocked at the destruction of the World Trade Center towers and the Pentagon? Have we not shown such evil plots and devastating destruction in Hollywood movies before? Is it not a case of sowing and reaping? Have we not played a part in sowing into the minds of terrorists?

If we want to nurture the spirit, we have to feed it with the things that are true, good, honorable, beautiful, noble, and praise-worthy.[4] We have to choose carefully everything we put into us— what we listen to, what we read, and what we watch. Thoughts are the seeds to words, deeds, and actions.

The most efficient way to feed our spirits with truth is through reading and meditating on the Scriptures. They are God's revelations of truth over the ages through many people. His written Word is the foundation for His spoken word into our spirits.

There is no substitute for finding the secret place of God's presence where we can find guidance through prayer and meditation. Because God is wise, we are enlightened in His presence. Because God is love, we are transformed into His love. Because God is truth, we are set free from our deceptions and delusions. Because God is perfect, we are perfected in His holy presence.

Then the spirit can soar and have the strength and wisdom to subdue the ego, take dominion over the mind, and subjugate the body as it seeks to live and respond to the divine will of God.

Endnotes

1. See John 4:24.
2. John 1:1.
3. Genesis 1:3.
4. See Philippians 4:8.

CHAPTER 4

IT'S WHO YOU KNOW

—● If I find Him, I will find myself
And if I find my true self, I will find Him.
(Thomas Merton) ●—

If you want to hear God…

SECRET #4: Get an introduction from someone in high places.

If you want to get a deal, it helps to know the business owner's son.

If you want to see the king, it helps to know the prince.

If you want to talk to God, you need an introduction from someone in high places.

You can approach Buddha, "the enlightened one," esteemed by many as a spiritual master who taught how to reach nirvana, the highest degree of "God-consciousness." You can observe Moses, who walked so closely to God that he was entrusted with the Ten Commandments and the Law. You can try understanding Muhammad, who speaks of the revelations from "Allah" written in the Koran. You can even try reading the words of Confucius, who wrote many classic books on ethics, morality, and social order in society.

These are all men who sought to understand the spiritual nature of the world we live in, and their writings have greatly impacted our world. There is only one problem—they are all dead, and their spirits have departed.

HE HAS NEVER WRITTEN ANYTHING; HE GAVE EVERYTHING

There is one other spiritual teacher you can still approach directly today. Though He has never written anything, He gave everything. You know the one—He was "resurrected" from the dead and appeared to hundreds of witnesses to prove that He was who He claimed to be—the Son of God, the Messiah, the Savior of the world.

He is a Jew named Jesus Christ. Do you know the meaning of His name? *Jesus* means "the Lord saves" and *Christ* means "the anointed One" in Greek. (The Hebrew word is *Messiah*.) After proving to His disciples without a shadow of a doubt that He was sent from God to save us and promising that He would give His Holy Spirit to anyone who believed, He returned to God, having completed His short mission on earth. Of all the other great teachers listed earlier, Jesus is the only one who came back from the dead as a "risen Savior." That is why He is the only one who is still alive today.

Now, even His apostles who witnessed the miracles He performed couldn't believe it when He came back from the grave. No one had ever come back from the dead! But then, Jesus wasn't just a man; He was God appearing in the form of man. He was divinity who descended into the body of humanity. That's why He called Himself Son of God *and* Son of Man.[1]

So, if you really want to talk to God, your best bet is to approach Jesus. Why? He alone can give you an introduction to God because He is really in high places—He is the Son; He is at the Father's side.

You are probably thinking that's not true. "How can a man be God? Jesus was a prophet like the others, but He was so deluded that He really thought He was God. That's why they killed Him."

Did you ever think that if you ask the wrong question, you would never find the right answer? The question is not, "How can a man be God?" but "Can God come in the form of man, if He chooses?"

Keep an open mind because you might be missing the whole point of who Jesus is and why God sent Him. God sent Him not only to teach us, but also to save us; not only to show the way, but also to *be* the way. This is the great difference between Jesus and all the other spiritual masters. He gives the power to become what He has declared. Jesus willingly accepted the crucifixion and served as the ultimate sacrifice for our sins. He died in our place so we could be saved and set free from our sins—from the errors, illusions, and delusions in our lives.

Set free to do what, you ask? Free to be reconciled to our Creator; free to have open communication with our Father as children of God; free to discern and become who God created us to be; and free to spend eternity with Him when our spirits depart from our bodies at the point of death.

"Since God is love and love is merciful, why couldn't He just overlook our offenses and forget all this business about the sacrifice, the blood, and the crucifixion?" you want to know.

Yes, God is love and God is merciful, but God is also fair and just.[2] Perfect love is as merciful as it is just. Without justice, there is no standard to judge anything. Without standards, there is no difference between right and wrong, good and evil.

"You mean God is going to judge us for our actions? I thought He was bigger than that! I thought He wasn't petty, critical, and judgmental like us."

God is not a petty tyrant; that is why He came up with this perfect plan to overlook our offenses without violating His justice. He provided the sacrifice Himself by coming in the form of humanity. He gave us a part of Himself, in the form of His only Son, because love is always giving and the heart of giving is sacrifice. The greater the love, the greater the gift and the greater the sacrifice.

God appeared in human form so we could finally understand Him. He had tried repeatedly to communicate to us through all His prophets, but we wouldn't listen. We killed them instead. So He came disguised as an ordinary carpenter so people from all races, all nations, and all ages could identify with Him. He spoke in parables and told simple stories so we could understand the invisible spiritual kingdom where we would eventually spend eternity with God.

Now, if you are Jewish, Muslim, Buddhist, or agnostic, you probably think I am trying to convert you. I am not. If what I am saying is truth, it will speak for itself. I was Jewish for sixteen years, and I have studied the Torah, the Koran, and many of the great eastern religions. I learned much that benefited me immeasurably. But it did not transform my heart, nor did it change the direction of my life.

I continued searching for God until one day I heard from God Himself. Then I "knew" the truth. I am only a witness to this truth hoping that you, too, can discover how to hear God yourself.

IT'S NOT WHAT YOU KNOW, BUT WHO YOU KNOW

Let's get back to the main point. If you want to hear God, you must first get into His presence. Now, it isn't that easy. God is a very important person. He's a VIP! Look at it this way. Have you ever tried to get a meeting with a CEO in order to try to land a job? How hard would that be?

But imagine if you knew the CEO's son…it makes all the difference, doesn't it? Especially if that son happens to be the chief operating officer and is willing to give dad a call. That would cut you through the red tape faster than you can say a prayer. *It's not what you know, but who you know that counts.*

It is the same with God. If you want to see God, you need an introduction from someone in high places. Go to Jesus. He told us that He is "the way and the truth and the life."[3] Are you still not convinced that this Jewish carpenter is really God Himself?

Why do you think the Roman Emperor Constantine himself—the head of the most powerful civilization in the world at that time—would eventually kneel down and worship this Jesus as the King of kings and Lord of lords?

Why do you suppose the definition of time in our world, in every nation and on every continent, is pegged to what Jesus did on the cross? Have you ever asked yourself why this is the year it is?

It is two thousand plus years after Jesus died on the cross.

The answer is simple—you can't destroy truth! Truth is true independent of what we think; it is not defined by our perceptions. Truth is a fact and a reality, and time always testifies to its authenticity. You can deny it, but you cannot change it.

WHY IS THERE A NEED FOR SACRIFICE?

You may think that the cross is a Christian concept, but it was originally a Roman form of torture and execution. Thousands were crucified on crosses. It is not the cross but the symbol of the sacrifice and the blood that is important to understand.

God's "blood of the covenant" required that blood be shed in order to obtain forgiveness of sin. Blood needed to be shed for the "atonement" of sins—in Hebrew, "to atone" is "to cover." The blood of the animal symbolized the covering of our sins before a holy God so we could enter into His holy presence and have communion with Him.

Since God made it clear that the penalty of sin is death and spiritual separation from Him, the animal symbolically took the sinner's place and paid the penalty for sin. Blood is the greatest representation of life. So this ancient practice of the Jewish people symbolized a life given so another life is saved. It required an unblemished animal to represent the moral perfection demanded by God.

This practice may seem repulsive to us today, but it was an effective way to teach about sin and repentance in the context of the Middle Eastern culture of that time. When people saw the sacrificial animal being killed and the life-blood flowing out of it, it convicted them of their own sin and guilt. They were reminded of their need for repentance and reconciliation with God.

Once a year, the high priest of Israel would seek God's forgiveness for the sins of the people during the Day of Atonement. He would sacrifice an unblemished animal like a lamb or a goat in order to enter into the Holy of Holies in the temple. That is the Most Holy Place, which symbolized the dwelling place of God's presence. The priest had to go through elaborate rituals to cleanse himself thoroughly by applying blood to parts of his body from head to toe.

In addition, the high priest had to camouflage himself with sweet smelling incense. Why? As sinners, no matter what we do, we don't smell too good to a perfectly holy God. Even the high priest didn't look too good to God, so he had to be disguised by the billowing cloud of smoke that covered him.

God has simplified everything with a "new covenant" because He wanted intimate and direct communion with all of His children. He provided both the sacrifice and the high priest so we could enter freely into His presence at any time. Jesus was that perfect, unblemished sacrifice of God that was offered on the cross. When He returned to Heaven, He became the high priest who ushers us into the presence of His Father.

GOD TOLD US SEVEN HUNDRED YEARS BEFORE

You may think this is all ancient myth and fable, but many of the details of the life of Jesus were prophesied by several Jewish prophets, like Isaiah, seven hundred years before—from His miraculous virgin birth to His cruel execution on the cross.

For example, Isaiah said, "The Lord Himself will give you a sign: The virgin will be with child and will give birth to a son, and will call Him Immanuel."[4] *Immanuel* means "God with us."

Jesus fulfilled not one, but thirty-three of these prophecies from God's promises in the Old Testament. The law of probability of anyone doing that as a coincidence is calculated to be in the trillions!

God told us that if we would believe Him, accept the precious gift of Jesus, turn from our evil ways, and repent sincerely, He would forgive us. We would be reconciled to Him instantly and completely, once and for all. Then we could enter into His presence and find the truth we need in order to live a godly life. We could commune with God directly and regularly, not just through a high priest once a year.

I don't know about you, but that is quite a deal—and without all the bloody mess and sacrifice. It is an ingenious plan that only a perfect God could devise for sinful people.

ASK GOD YOURSELF

If you are tired of hearing other people's hand-me-down, secondhand revelations, shouldn't you find God and talk to Him directly yourself? That's what I did. He will give you the answer to the question, "What is truth?"

So if you want to see God and you've been given the runaround and are really tired of being in the waiting room, try talking to His Son Jesus first. He can cut through the line and usher you in because He is really in high places—He is the high priest Himself. You don't have to bribe Him, either; He will do it freely because God wants to see you. Really!

He did that for me and countless other people. It works, I guarantee you! Don't worry, I am not talking about accepting a new religion or joining a church. This is only about how to get through to God.

Go ahead and try it! What have you got to lose? God might even talk to you.

Endnotes

1. See John 10:36; Matthew 16:13, et. al.
2. See 1 John 4:16; Psalm 116:5; Isaiah 45:21.
3. John 14:6.
4. Isaiah 7:14.

CHAPTER 5

HURRY UP AND WAIT!

If you want to hear God's voice clearly and you are uncertain, then remain in His presence until He changes this uncertainty. Often much can happen during this waiting for the Lord. Sometimes He changes pride into humility; doubts into faith and peace...

(Corrie ten Boom)

If you want to hear God...

Secret #5: Wait on God patiently and show Him that you are serious about hearing Him.

"How do I learn patience, God?" I asked.

"*Wait upon Me, son,*" He replied.

"How long must I wait?" I continued.

"*Until you are ready,*" God said.

"How long will that be?" I pressed on.

"*Until you stop asking,*" He said.

"What can I do now?" I questioned.

"*Hurry up and wait!*" God responded.

(A dialogue from my spiritual journal)

If you want to hear God, you have to find a way to get through to Him. After all, He is God...the Chief...the CEO of CEOs! Even if you get an introduction, you still have to wait. So what do you *do* while you are waiting?

THE QUALITY OF OUR WAITING

I have done a lot of waiting on God in the past ten years. During those countless hours, days, and weeks of waiting, fasting, and praying, I discovered a simple truth: The quality of our waiting determines the excellence of our visitation with God.

Waiting is the process that silences the meaningless chatter in our souls so we can hear God.

Waiting focuses the mind and quiets the spirit. It clarifies our purpose and cleanses our motives.

It stretches our patience and perfects our perseverance. Waiting allows time to extinguish the flame of desire and release our attachments to the things of this world.

Waiting nourishes our spirits and strengthens our faith. It purifies our hearts and elevates our souls.

It helps us find the path to the secret chamber of our souls. In this invisible and eternal world of the spirit, we enter into a secret place where we can experience the holy presence of God.

No wonder God told us to hurry up and learn how to wait. He can't wait to see us!

If you have been granted a meeting with the President of the United States, the most powerful political leader in the world, would you casually walk in without any purpose or preparation? That is exactly what many people do with God. That's why they don't hear God, and yet they wonder why. It's because they have not demonstrated the pressure of purpose and the desperation of desire.

In our Internet age, we have no patience. We are intolerant of any delay. We hate to wait. We want everything now! Faster is better. We expect instant communication and constant gratification. It is the "Just Do It" generation that can't wait to do something. We want to download God with a touch of the computer keyboard, now!

LEARNING HOW TO WAIT

I have a little secret for you: If you really want to hear God, you must learn how to wait on Him first. Jesus waited and fasted forty days in the wilderness. Moses waited forty years in the desert. Daniel of the Old Testament prayed for twenty-one days straight. No wonder they all heard from God and received so many revelations.

All the great men and women who sought God throughout history have understood the gateway to the spiritual life. To hear God, we have to prepare ourselves through prayer, fasting, and meditation while we wait. Why? This essential preparation calibrates our hearing and heightens our spiritual tuner so we can hear God.

Waiting is the time when we empty ourselves so we can be filled. God can't fill us if we are full of self.

So what do we *do* while we wait?

I was one of the most impatient people in the world. I was always on the go, and I got my share of speeding tickets, too. My life and career were always in fast motion. I could never sit still for a moment because I never wanted to waste time. I thought waiting was just killing time, so I got anxious and irritable when I was forced to wait.

A REVELATION FROM GOD

In a prayer and meditation session on Saturday, November 12, 1994, I asked God to help me understand this subject of patience. I was going through a very stressful period at the time and faced many trials because of a possible transition in my career. I was constantly worrying and speculating on what to do.

Finally, I asked God to give me clear guidance and specific direction. "Please, God, tell me what to *do*...now!"

Then God spoke.

"Dear son, when you are waiting, turn away from wishing and wanting. Turn from anxiety and anger; run away from impatience and intolerance, and you will be relieved from trials and tribulations.

"Focus instead on worshiping, anticipating, introspecting, and thanksgiving.

"As you focus on Me and My will, the mist of doubt, the fog of confusion, and the smoke of stress will lift. Your eyes will see clearly as the truth is revealed.

"Your faith will blow away the mist, the fog, and the smoke. Your prayers will be answered, for My will cannot be denied."

After hearing God, my anxieties and fears started to subside, and a sense of peace and comfort descended on me. How had this happened? I had just wanted God to give me a simple answer on what to *do* about my immediate circumstances. I needed to make a decision, but God had a different perspective—His thoughts are not our thoughts and His ways are not our ways.[1]

God is always looking at the bigger picture because He can see the end from the beginning. God is always more concerned with who we *are* than what we *do*.

When God speaks to us, it often seems like He does not give us the simple answers we want. He stretches our minds to understand and enlarges our vision to see the larger spiritual principles from an eternal perspective. Like a master teacher, He seldom gives simplistic answers to complex questions; rather, He prefers to engage us in higher thinking by asking another question. This forces the student to stop, think, and learn.

That is why I write down everything I hear in a spiritual journal. More often than not, it is necessary to read over again and meditate on what God has spoken to me to seek further illumination. When it comes to hearing God, it is vital that we correctly and effectively interpret the words we hear in order to avoid fatal mistakes.

It was only after I reread what God said that I realized God's play on the letters in the word *wait*: wishing and wanting, anxiety and anger, impatience and intolerance, trials and tribulations.

Then there is this one: worshiping, anticipating, introspecting, and thanksgiving.

As I sat there and meditated on His words, He began to give me fresh revelations on His words.

In the beginning of my journey, when I heard people praying and praising God and going on and on with eloquent words worshiping God, I used to wonder, *Why is God so egotistical that He makes us all bow down and worship Him?*

WORSHIP

Then, in this meditation session, God showed me that He didn't need our worship; it is really for our benefit. When we worship God, we are not exalting Him; God is already exalted. We are not magnifying Him, for He is already infinite.

We need to worship God because it aligns our minds and focuses our spirits on the truth and reality of God. Worshiping God exalts our spirits and magnifies our faith so we can be spiritually sensitive to detect the presence of God. Worshiping God helps usher us into His presence, which provides the proper perspective to understanding the totality of life.

As our faith rises, we begin to sense the presence of God inside us, outside us, and everywhere!

The truth is, God is omnipresent; He is always present... everywhere! Worship simply helps us tune in to His presence by acknowledging the truth of who He is and praising Him for what He has done.

For example, worship could be saying, "Almighty God, there is none like You. You are a God of infinite love and mercy—all power and authority are in Your hands; nothing is impossible with You. Thank You for Your love, protection, and provision. I love You with all my heart and soul, and I dedicate this day to You."

Worship nourishes our spirits with the truth of God and feeds our minds with the reality of God. It opens our hearts to receive His love and prepares our spirits to hear His will. Worship is one of the doorways we can use to enter the secret place where we encounter the holy presence of God's Spirit. Worship lifts us up out of the despair of our life and into the depths of God's love.

When we hear God, His word reveals truth. In the presence of light, we are enlightened—we receive revelation knowledge. Suddenly, everything is revealed, and it all makes sense! Truth takes off the blinders of our preconceived perception and reveals the true state of reality.

It is as if a light has just been turned on in a dark room where we have been groping around trying to find something we had lost. Revelation is the light turned on in our darkness so that we know how to respond. Turning on the light of revelation helps us put the power of truth in action, which sets us free from the errors of our ways.

Worshiping is God-centered, not self-centered; it helps us align our will to His and cancels our deceptions as His truth is revealed. The reason so many people are not hearing God is because they don't know how to worship. Their prayers have become self-centered wishing and wanting, groveling and bargaining, negotiating and bribing sessions with God.

I made all these mistakes in my journey as I sought God. That's why I am sharing these things with you. God is not offended by our ignorance, but self-centered worship won't usher us into His presence. So how can we hear Him to receive the revelations we need? How can we claim the ultimate blessing—the blessing that comes from His spoken words?

ANTICIPATE

If you have an appointment with the President of the United States, you have a reason, purpose, and objective for the meeting. You are excited about this great opportunity; you anticipate and plan the visit long before your scheduled appointment. In your anticipation, you rehearse every possible detail you can think of. Why? Because you respect the position of the presidency, and you want to make the best of the president's time.

You would do all the necessary research to find out what is currently on the president's agenda. Then you would target your request to his stated priorities and what he is already doing. You formulate your opening compliments and thank him for seeing you. You would praise him for what he has done and what he is doing to make a better country and a better world. You anticipate and rehearse your questions and requests. You would do anything to make the best impression and achieve your ultimate purpose.

Would you do any less with God?

If we want to have a quality encounter with God, we must prepare ourselves in anticipation. God keeps us waiting not to frustrate us, but to give us time to prepare for and focus on the purpose and outcome of the meeting.

This waiting period is time well spent on understanding God's plan and priorities. It is time to align our will to His will.

Even God can't help us if we don't know what we want or need. We must ask because God won't force anything on us. When we know what we need and why we need it, then God will provide it in His perfect timing—if it is good for us and for the greater good of all. Waiting refines our wants and needs, preparing us to ask and receive from God.

INTROSPECTION

Introspection is when we look at ourselves, inside the deepest recesses of our hearts, to see if there is anything we need to clean up before our visit with God. If we want to get into God's presence, then we have to first clean ourselves up spiritually. Why?

You wouldn't go to Buckingham Palace to see Queen Elizabeth looking like a bum, would you? The security guards would probably arrest you. No, you would clean yourself up and look your very best because you respect the dignity of the office. You appreciate the fact that the queen has taken time out of her hectic schedule to see you.

God is holy and perfect in every way; He is morally perfect, and we are not. He is right all of the time, and we are not. If we want to develop a right relationship with Him, then we have to learn how to come into His presence.

God does not expect us to come in perfection, but in honesty. Since none of us is perfect, we have to humbly acknowledge this truth. We must confess that we have missed the mark of His design for our lives. Our confession is transformed into sorrowful repentance. No matter what it is, God already knows about it because He is omniscient and all knowing. We have nothing to be fearful about because God loves us. He simply wants us to acknowledge the truth. He wants us to show a willingness to change by accepting His unconditional love and forgiveness, and try again.

When we examine ourselves in introspection and then confess and repent, it is not for God's benefit. It is for our benefit, so we won't hide from God because of guilt and shame. Guilt and shame are the two tyrants that will keep you from God. God is not a sadistic, petty tyrant who enjoys judging us when we are on our knees before Him. No, when we align ourselves to the truth of our sinful condition and sincerely ask God for forgiveness and help, He always will. It is in God's nature to forgive because He is merciful and His love is unconditional.

THANKSGIVING

Thanksgiving is the heart's response to a loving God. If we have gone through the steps of worshiping, anticipating, and introspection, they automatically lead us to a far greater appreciation of God. Gratitude flows out of our hearts like a stream of thanksgiving. It shoots out of our spirits like a fountain of praise.

I remember the few times when my thanksgiving really touched the heart of God. Once I wrote a song entitled "None Like You" and sang it to Him. Another time I wrote a poem called "Without You."

Then there was a time when I wrote a psalm to God. Now I am writing this book as another way to give thanks to Him.

I also keep a prayer list and a miracle list in the back of my spiritual journals. It is my scorecard with God. After all, the bottom line to prayer is answered prayers. Otherwise, what is the point in wasting all our time? I mark off the answered prayers as I go. The miracle list contains things in my life that are above and beyond anything I prayed for or imagined, such as a miraculous healing or unexpected blessing.

This is my account book with God. It reconciles everything like an accountant balances the books. It helps me recognize God's faithfulness over time. When I am sick and my body is dragging from catching a cold, I reread my old journals. Instantly I am reminded of a simple truth: God hears me and answers prayers! It might not always be in my timing or in my way, but He answers prayers. I am reminded once again that delay is not denial.

Thanksgiving is a process by which you acknowledge the truth and the reality of what God has done in your life and in the world. You would be surprised at how much He is doing in your life and in the world if you would stop and meditate on it. Too often we miss the little miracles God does every day because we don't take the time to reflect back.

I remember the time when I prayed this prayer of thanksgiving before our guests before dinner:

"Dear God, we are thankful for our friends. We are thankful for Your love. We are thankful for this colorful paella dish. It's a miracle how these green mussels from New Zealand, shrimps from the Gulf of Mexico, clams from Manila, and rice from Thailand all ended up in this one dish. How wonderful You are, oh God. We thank You for this and for all the miracles in our lives that we take for granted every day."

A MIRACLE HEALING OF MY WIFE

The ultimate expression of faith is when you thank God for something you asked for, before you receive it. Faith is the substance of what you hope for and the evidence of what you have not seen yet.[2] In the spirit world, it has already been granted, but you must wait for it to manifest in the physical world—if you have the faith to act upon it.

Let me try to explain using the story of the miraculous healing of my wife, Tere. The doctor had diagnosed her with a growing tumor in her breast that required an operation right away. The X-ray clearly showed a disturbing growth. Instead we went to a healing service at our church and asked God for healing. The elders anointed her with oil while the whole group prayed and told her to postpone the operation until God fully healed her. She obeyed, canceled the appointment, and thanked God for the healing in advance.

A month later, when she went in for another biopsy, the nurse could not find a trace of the lump. Incredulous, the nurse placed Tere onto another machine, but she still found no trace. How could this be? The nurse called in the doctor, and they compared the X-rays from before, in which the lump was clearly visible and marked. There was no scientific explanation—it was a miracle! You should have seen their faces when they had to write the letter to explain my wife's new condition.

What you would not believe is this: God had spoken to me about a miracle several weeks before, and I wrote it in my journal. He promised me that there would be a miracle as one of three confirmations to my question of whether or not we should move to Los Angeles.

You see, I had been offered the opportunity to be CEO of both the Dream Center and City Help, which serve the hurting, the helpless, and the hopeless in the inner city of Los Angeles. At the time we were not aware of Tere's tumor, so I assumed the miracle would be the healing of my back injury. For ten years after a traumatic car accident, I had been plagued with back pain, and I had been praying for healing for a long time.

When we went to our church's healing service, we were both hoping for our healing and praying for each other. But, Tere had so much faith that it never occurred to her that she would not be healed. She thanked God ahead of time and postponed the operation, despite the doctor's advice.

God also knew that Tere did not want to move to L.A., where I would work in a dangerous, gang-infested neighborhood. At the time we were living in a beautiful house with a pool in Scottsdale, Arizona. God had to do something dramatic to get her attention. Needless to say, He got Tere's attention, and we moved to Los Angeles.

THE GREATER MIRACLE

What we didn't expect was how God would use us to bless others there in L.A. He used me to launch City Help, as the founding CEO. We developed a shelter for those who were dying of AIDS, a wellness center, and a forty-foot mobile medical truck, which provided free medical help to the poor and homeless who were without access to any medical attention.

Following God's direction, the Dream Center eliminated its $1.35 million debt in just three months. We were able to increase our outreach to the children, prostitutes, gangs, runaway youths, and drug addicts in the city. With God's help, we touched the lives of more than thirty-five thousand people every week.

During his presidential election campaign, George W. Bush came to the Dream Center to deliver his faith-based message. He praised co-founders Pastor Tommy and his son Pastor Mathew Barnett for rallying the armies of compassion. The *New York*

Times featured the Dream Center on its front pages twice during my first year there. What a miracle! And it all began by hearing God and trusting Him.

Today, more than a hundred Dream Centers have spread all over the country and around the world. I was blessed to have had the opportunity to serve as the first CEO.

Tere, on the other hand, volunteered as a teacher, serving the poorest Hispanic children in a school in McArthur Park—one of the most dangerous, drug-infested neighborhoods in Los Angeles.

One day I came home and couldn't find room in the garage to park my car, it was so packed with colorful presents. It was the end of the school year, and the parents wanted to express the depth of their appreciation for what Tere had done for their children. So my wife reaped what she had sowed. God chose to use her there because she was once an immigrant child from Colombia, just like them. God had healed Tere so she could heal others.

GOD HEALS US SO WE CAN HEAL OTHERS

God's ways are not our ways.[3] He has a way of rearranging our plans and our lives for the greater good, if we are willing to listen and obey. And He heals us so we can heal others.

God does not need our praise and thanksgiving, even though He enjoys it like parents enjoy hearing it from their children. *We* need to offer thanksgiving in order to align our minds and spirits to the truth and reality of what God has done. It reminds us of His power and provision, of His grace and faithfulness. It strengthens our faith and lifts our spirits. It prepares us to enter into His holy presence for another encounter with God.

My last piece of advice on this topic is, don't overdo it with prayers. If you really want to hear God, stop talking so much. Few of us understand the listening side of prayer. He already knows what you are going to say. Start listening instead. God is polite; He won't interrupt you if you insist on doing all the talking.

God has many ways of communicating, and He can manifest His presence through physical and other miracles so we can experience Him. Let these testimonies inspire you to seek God and wait upon Him so you, too, can hear Him.

As you perfect the quality of your waiting, you will improve the excellence of your visitation. You will learn to hear God more clearly over time as you develop a loving relationship with Him.

Endnotes

1. See Isaiah 55:8.
2. See Hebrews 11:1.
3. See Isaiah 55:8.

CHAPTER 6

JUST SAY YES!

⬤──── If indeed cry out for insight, and raise your voice for understanding,

If you seek it like silver, and search for is as hidden treasures,

Then you will understand the fear of the Lord and find knowledge of God.

(Proverbs 2:3-5) ────⬤

If you want to hear God...

SECRET #6: Seek holiness, and He will make you whole.

"Son, if you can have any three things you want, what would you ask of Me?" God whispered.

"Holiness, holiness, and holiness!" I replied without hesitation.

> *"Because you asked for holiness, I will make you whole. Because you didn't ask for anything else, I will give you everything else,"* God concluded.

(An excerpt from my spiritual journal)

A REVELATION ON THE MEANING OF HOLINESS

I used to think that only saints were "holy." I believed that holiness was some kind of peculiar spiritual DNA that God placed into certain people, like the special physical endowments He puts into the bodies of great athletes. I thought that to be holy, you had to give up everything in the world, live in a monastery, pray continually, and seek God. All of that would count me out— I didn't want to be so heavenly minded that I would be doing no earthly good.

One day God gave me a revelation: Saints are just sinners like me; the difference is they have never stopped trying to be holy. *Holiness is just another fancy word for whole. If we seek holiness, God will make us whole...and holy.*

Holy cow! I thought. (Pardon the pun.) *What a deal! God would do it for me?*

I was so excited, I asked God, "How?"

He replied, *"I will correct your erroneous thinking, which is caused by sin."*

Like the mysterious word *holy*, *sin* is another one of those intimidating words that scares people away from God. However, it simply means missed the mark, crossed the line, or wandered off the path from God's perfect will.

When we seek holiness, we are asking God to help correct our errors and show us how to hit the bull's-eye of His perfect will for us. God's will is always for us to be whole, complete, and lacking nothing, like Him. That's holy!

Since people are made in God's image, then we were made whole originally. God is perfect, and you don't think a perfect God would make defective parts, do you? Sin introduced errors into our thinking like a computer virus does to a computer system.

Wrong Thinking Leads to Wrong Doing

Wrong thinking gives birth to wrong doing. Wrong actions cause wrong reactions, and the chain of events keeps multiplying unless the thinking is corrected. For example, racism is based on a single mistaken thought that some races are superior to others. It led to misguided national policies that, in turn, resulted in disastrous actions with horrific consequences. Racism caused slavery and the genocide of millions of innocent victims—and it all began with an erroneous thought.

Jealousy, envy, and covetousness all start with the wrong thought of comparing oneself to others.

Greed starts with the erroneous thought of lack instead of abundance. *If we believe we are whole, we know we have everything and are everything we are meant to be. If we know we are whole, we will stop grasping and start giving. We will stop chasing blessings and start being a blessing.*

All of us have undetected viruses in our thought systems. We have our blind spots. They are called blind spots because we cannot see them. So we go through life with these blind areas judging others with prejudices that we don't even recognize. We evaluate everything based on our incomplete and inaccurate databases. We pre-judge situations using partial truth. (Remember, that's where the word *prejudice* came from.)

When we seek holiness, we are asking God to correct our "stinking thinking" based on generations of faulty programming. Such thinking is the product of our environments and of errors passed on from generation to generation, sometimes by parents and the very culture we are raised in.

Why We Need to Seek and Hear God

We need to seek and hear God because He is the source of absolute truth. He alone can purify our thinking until our thoughts are pure, perfect, right, and without error. When our consciousness is restored to its original, wholesome state, we will know the truth that sets us free from our sins.

We will know that God loves us. We are made in the image of our divine Creator, and He loves everyone and everything He created. We are brothers and sisters of the same human family. We can love one another as God loves us.

When we are made whole in our thinking, we automatically become holy in our actions. Correct thinking gives birth to right conduct. When we do what is right, we are righteous. We are in right standing with God, friends who are always welcomed into His holy presence at any time.

The important concept here is this: *God is the only one who can help make us holy. As our Creator, He alone can make us whole again if we ask for His help. We can try to make ourselves whole until we are blue in the face, but an error is incapable of correcting its own mistake.* That's why we need to hear from God. It's like downloading the right software to correct the viruses in our system. Exposing ourselves to God is the key to our healing and hearing, not running from Him because of our pride and shame.

WHAT WOULD YOU ASK OF GOD?

Over the years, God has asked me this question on three separate occasions: *"Son, if you can have any three things you want, what would you ask of Me?"* My answer was different each time. The first time, I really had to ponder the question. Then I said, "Obedience, obedience, and obedience." The second time, I asked for "humility, humility, and humility" because I learned that humility leads to obedience.

When God asked me a third time, I answered without hesitation, "Holiness, holiness, and holiness." By that time, I realized that holiness encompasses everything else that I lacked. I needed holiness so I could be made whole! And God responded,

"Because you asked for holiness, I will make you whole. Because you didn't ask for anything else, I will give you everything else."

PERSISTENCE IS EVERYTHING

In my walk with God, I discovered the truth of the Scripture, *"Ask and it will be given to you; seek and you will find; knock and the door will be opened to you."*[1] If you really want to hear from God, you have to ask and keep on asking! You have to seek and keep on seeking! You have to knock and keep on knocking! God wants to make sure we are sincere about what we want, and keeping us waiting exposes the sincerity of the desires of our hearts.

At first you will seek Him to help you get out of trouble. Then you will ask Him to bless you with what you think you need. As you develop more intimacy with God, your desires are refined and eventually all you will desire is to be bathed in the light and glory of His holy presence.

> *Once you know that the greatest spiritual treasures God can give you are knowledge of Himself and the wisdom that comes from Him, you will stop seeking His hands and start seeking His face. You will stop chasing His presents and start craving His presence.*

If you seek sincerely, then before long the door will open and God will speak to you. He will even ask you questions like He asked me. A two-way dialogue will begin, centered in a loving relationship with Him. It takes time, commitment, effort, and trust to develop any intimate relationship, though. So let me repeat that, ultimately, your ability to hear and experience God depends on the quality of your relationship with Him.

BE CAREFUL WHAT YOU ASK FOR

Now, be careful what you ask for because God will give you the desires of your heart, if those desires are good for you. And sometimes those things might not come in the forms that you expect. Let me tell you what I got when I asked for humility.

"How can I serve You, God?" I asked.

"*When you develop humility, son,*" He replied.

"How do I learn humility?" I continued.

"*When you are humiliated,*" God replied.

This is the last step of humility. There are other ways; for instance, you can learn humility in the presence of God without being humiliated. Unfortunately, it is true that the humiliation of life does bring humility.

When I was a child, my mom always thought I was strong-willed. I was not like my other three siblings. Whenever I was locked up in a room as punishment, I would not passively sit there and cry. Instead, I literally would climb the walls and try to escape out the tiny windows on top.

Over the years, as I ascended the ladder of success, my strong will grew stronger. I became increasingly more self-assured, self-centered, and egotistical—all ingredients of pride. I was an intensely independent thinker who heard a different drummer and marched to a different beat.

These are hardly qualities that would make me obedient to authority, and God is the ultimate authority. So when I asked for humility, God first had to teach me how to be humble to the visible authority He had placed over me on earth. We can't submit to an invisible heavenly Master if we won't humble ourselves before our earthly masters.

PRICELESS LESSONS IN SUBMISSION

It was the year 1993. I was at the top of my field as a young, visionary leader in public broadcasting. I was hopping around the world holding press conferences and drumming up "global partners to produce global programs for a global era." That was our slogan and stated strategy. I had the support of the board, a good relationship with the governor, and ample funding from the U.S. Congress and the Maryland state legislature.

The *Washington Post*'s TV magazine featured me on the front cover with a story entitled, "The World Is His Market Place." *USA Today* ran an article praising me, called, "Selling Quality In Syndication." Our "Motorweek" show hit the front of *Variety*, the most influential magazine in showbiz.

But, in God's economy, none of that impressed Him the least bit. We are most vulnerable when we are at the top of the mountain because that's where we are most susceptible to *pride*—the AIDS of the soul. If God was going to teach me humility, He had to cure me of this spiritual disease.

I was about to begin my downhill descent into the valley of humiliation where I discovered new valleys beyond every valley. I went from the heat of the kitchen into the frying pan and then into the fire. I was burned to ashes before God could remake me.

He told me, "*Son, I have to deform you before I can reform you and conform you.*" Little did I know the tests, trials, and tribulations I was going to endure next. (But then, without those tests, there would be no testimony, and I wouldn't be writing this book.)

No Way to Escape God's Discipline

First, remember how I told you He used Tere, my second wife, to bring me to my knees? During my first sixteen years of marriage, I always got my way because my first wife was very passive. Tere is the opposite. She knows exactly what she wants and when she wants it on everything!

Suddenly, the CEO had to submit to a new CEO at home. It was...very humbling, to say the least.

Then, on top of that, I got a domineering new boss at work, too! God really has a sense of humor. Have you noticed He often uses people whom we can't get rid of easily in our lives to force us to change? That's what He meant when He said, "I will make you whole and holy"—and there is no way to escape.

While I was with the Maryland PBS network, the governor appointed a new chairman to our board. Our new chairman was an impressive man; he was a Harvard Law School graduate, a partner in one of the largest law firms in Baltimore, a prominent citizen, and a close friend of the governor.

With all his credentials and connections, our chairman was like me—strong-willed, demanding, controlling, and, yes, egotistical! From day one, he was going to change everything. He was going to change the direction of the network and refocus its programming from global to local—which was diametrically opposed to everything I had done. God really knows how to turn up the heat.

First, he appointed a particular gentleman to head up an evaluation committee of the board to assess my performance. Now, I was not born yesterday. I immediately knew why he appointed a distinguished African-American to be the hatchet man. This gentleman was a former chancellor of a university and a highly respected leader in the African-American community. There was no way for me to challenge the validity of his evaluation based on racial discrimination.

Surprise! For the first time in my professional career, I got a bad evaluation. It wasn't just bad; it was horrible. It stunk! I was incensed, and my ego was absolutely devastated. I wanted to fight and challenge the validity of the evaluation because it was highly subjective. I knew I could win on the merits of the facts.

I prayed and asked God for guidance, hoping that He would show me how to combat this situation. But, to my disappointment, He said, "*Raymond, I don't want you to do that. Instead, use the evaluation as a way to develop humility. Use it as a grindstone to sharpen your obedience.*"

OBEDIENCE BEGINS BY SAYING "YES"

Obedience to God always begins by saying "yes"! If God speaks to you, remember to "just say yes." No matter where you are, say yes, for it opens your heart to Him. So when this esteemed African-American asked me whether I wanted a meeting with the committee to discuss my evaluation, I obeyed God and politely declined. I think he was surprised.

Then God kept turning up the heat day after day, month after month. At every board meeting, I would be thoroughly humiliated under the heavy hand of the chairman. Usually the lay chairman would welcome the board members and the CEO would conduct the meeting. This new chairman changed the rules and ran the show himself.

He would bypass me and ask my senior vice presidents to answer his questions. Like a good lawyer, he would cross-examine to make a convincing case to the board that all the international productions were unprofitable. Ironically, the network's revenues had grown steadily during my tenure, and now he was demanding "profitability" in a non-profit sector. That was a first!

To turn up the heat so I would get out of the kitchen, our chairman changed the quarterly meetings to monthly meetings. This, too, was God's way of giving me what I had asked for. He speeded up my lessons in humility by increasing my tolerance for humiliation. It was during this period in the furnace of affliction that I first developed an intense prayer life. That was when I started seeking God desperately, which gave birth to my spiritual journals.

Only God Knows How Much We Can Take

One day, just when I was ready to crack up and break, everything changed. Since I had obeyed God, He knew exactly how much I could take, and He wasn't going to test me beyond my ability to bear.[2] God didn't want to break me. He wanted to test me, cut me down to size, and teach me submission to authority.

That day, the gentleman who had headed up the evaluation committee said he would consider coming to work for me as senior vice president of programming. That was the division that was under pressure by the new chairman.

I thought to myself, *Is this God? Or is this the devil disguised as an angel of light?*

It turned out to be a miracle reward for my obedience. God gave me the only thing that could help me survive the heat of the furnace. This gentleman became my asbestos suit! He had been on the board for ten years and had many friends in high places. If there were any hidden problems in that division, he would surely bring it to the attention of the board. More than that, this gentleman would fix them.

This frustrated our chairman to no end. It was the last thing he had expected. However, my furnace wasn't over yet.

One day, an assistant attorney general came to see me with a long, sober face. He said, "I am very sorry to tell you this bad news, but the chairman asked me to do an investigation on you. A staff member alleged that you have violated the constitutional rights of the staff by praying in a staff meeting."

I was shocked and stunned. I said, "That's a lie! I know about separation of church and state, and I have never made anyone pray."

"Do you have any proof, Raymond?" the assistant attorney general asked.

I was at a loss on how to prove something that didn't happen. Then suddenly I remembered that the staff meetings were always recorded on tape, so I submitted the tape to be transcribed. It proved that I had requested a moment of silence when we were forced by the state cutbacks to lay off a dozen people. There was no prayer.

The days and months dragged on as I camped out at the bottom of my valley of despair. My hair was turning white fast. I was like a prisoner suffering from the Chinese torture of dripping water (read, humiliation!) that caused great agony to my soul. Day after day, I kept begging God, bribing God, and negotiating for my release.

After a year had passed, the chairman pressed for another performance evaluation.

I said to God, "Oh please, not another one! I can't take it anymore!"

This evaluation committee was chaired by yet another prominent African-American. By then I knew the drill. This lady was a former assistant superintendent of education with a humble spirit. Having seen my newfound humility at the board meetings, though, she was sympathetic. She also was a friend of my new senior vice president of programming, who had chaired my evaluation the year before. That made a big difference.

To my amazement, my evaluation was good! However, that was totally unacceptable to our chairman. In my view, he was looking for a way to put the final nail in my coffin—and to do it, that evaluation needed to be changed.

TOTAL SURRENDER AND SUBMISSION

At that point, I totally gave up bargaining and groveling with God. I finally learned to give up, give in, surrender, and submit totally to His will.

Then God spoke. *"Son, do not fear. When you obey Me, I will protect you. If you are humble and truthful, there is no need to defend yourself. Anyone who attacks you would only hurt himself."*

Sure enough, the head of the evaluation committee stood her ground. My good evaluation remained. But, the more the chairman pushed, the more the board resisted. Until one day, the ultimate humiliation came…not for me, but for the chairman.

A new governor had been elected, and he appointed his own chairman. The governor also asked our chairman to step down, before the end of his term. This was unprecedented because it was customary to let the outgoing chairman finish his term with dignity unless he chose to step down on his own.

The chairman who had been like a thorn in my side might have been headstrong, but he was devoted to the cause of public broadcasting and did not deserve such humiliation. But then, perhaps God was teaching him, too. God was using both of us to refine each other on our pilgrim's journey.

FORGIVENESS IS A TRUE SIGN OF ENLIGHTENMENT

Then one day God said, "I want you to forgive that chairman and show him you love him."

Forgiveness is a true sign of enlightenment; it is through forgiveness that we perfect love. There was nothing for me to forgive because who was I to judge? I obeyed God and planned a wonderful farewell party for the outgoing chairman.

When I told him about the event, he asked me, "Why are you doing this?"

I replied, "Because it is the right thing to do. It's always good to do the right thing."

During his farewell speech, the chairman exhibited a gentler and humbler side. He touched everyone with his remarks and concluded by saying, "Raymond, I have learned a lot from you."

I thought, *Oh no, not from me. We are both students and prisoners at the foot of the Master.*

I was so thankful for what God had done. As I rejoiced, I knew that hearing God is the ultimate blessing and that obeying Him leads to miracles. Little did I know that I was about to go from the frying pan into the fire, since I had asked for so much of God...obedience, humility, and holiness.

Endnotes

1. Matthew 7:7.
2. See 1 Corinthians 10:13.

CHAPTER 7

JUST DO IT!

> Do you know the voice of God? Can we be led by the voice? Have we the faith that can Follow when the path seems so strangely crooked? ...It is a splendid abandonment of the will of another...a "holy recklessness" as to the consequences...but if He calls...FOLLOW.
>
> **(George Soltau)**

If you want to hear God...

SECRET #7: Obey, and you will experience the miracle power of truth in action. Disobey, and you will miss your ultimate blessing.

"Dear God, how do I obey You?" I asked.

"Just do what I tell you to do when I tell you to do it," He replied.

"How do I know it is You talking to me?" I continued.

"When you finish doubting, come back and ask Me again," God said.

"I am finished doubting…but how can I be sure that my doubts are not true?"

"Just do it!" He concluded.

(A dialogue from my spiritual journal)

STRUGGLING AND CONQUERING DOUBTS

Faith and doubt are like two sides of the same coin. Without doubt there is no need for faith. You cannot have one without the other. In the spirit world, if doubt is like the darkness of the unknown, then faith is like the light that reveals the known. You cannot develop faith until you have struggled with and conquered your doubts. How do you do this?

My advice is this: If God speaks to you, follow His instructions right away and "just do it!"

When you obey, you will experience the miraculous power of truth in action. If you doubt and disobey, you will miss your ultimate blessing.

When I told my brother about my experiences with hearing God, he said, "If I heard a voice speaking to me and it was not from a physical source, I would check myself into a mental hospital."

But then, he is a dentist. As a trained scientist, he has a hard time accepting the intangible concept of faith.

I find it very interesting when people say that they don't have enough faith to believe in God, let alone hear from God.

Let me ask you this: "With all the news stories about hijackings and plane crashes, do you have faith that your airline is going to get you to your destination?"

"Yes, of course!" you answer.

"How do you know?"

"Based on the record of the airline and personal experience," you say.

"But how do you know, for example, that your plane doesn't have a mechanical problem?"

"I don't know for sure," you conclude.

"Then you have faith!" I say.

EVERYONE HAS A MEASURE OF FAITH

Faith is not a mysterious spiritual gift that God has placed only in certain people He has chosen to do His work. Everyone has a measure of faith, even if it is as small as a mustard seed.[1] Faith is just another word for trust or confidence.

When we have faith in God, what we are saying is simply this: "God, I believe that Your word is true, You are who You say You are, and You will do what You say You will do."

Faith is based on trust in God's word because His word is His bond. We trust what we have "experienced" and have confidence in what we "know." Faith is built on the foundation of experience.

When we were children, we had no problem with the concept of faith; we trusted and loved our parents and everyone else. Why? Because we were born with faith, we had no reason to doubt. We were not yet contaminated by the paralyzation of fear.

As we grow up, we experience fear. By experience we become distrustful toward others. We learn to be suspicious of people's motives. We learn to doubt their goodness. Our doubt then turns inward as we start doubting ourselves. Unfounded insecurities begin to form. Over time, we internalize this experience of disbelief in ourselves and in others. We lose that wonderful quality called faith that we were born with.

If money is the medium that makes the visible world go round, then faith is the spiritual currency that moves mountains in the invisible world. Faith and obedience go hand in hand, and without faith we cannot please God.[2]

The way you demonstrate faith is through obedience, and the way to show obedience is through action...just do it! Then the power of God's truth is set into motion and you begin to experience the miraculous. You receive your ultimate blessing through obedience that is empowered by faith in God's word.

THE OPPOSITE OF FAITH IS FEAR

The opposite of faith is fear. When fear is "pregnant," it gives birth to doubts. Unbelief is demonstrated by doubting God and fearing to do what He tells you. Then you miss your ultimate blessing through disobedience.

> *God is the source of truth. When He speaks, He illuminates our minds, opens our spiritual eyes, and infuses our hearts with truth. The circle of faith can be completed only if we choose to believe and obey Him.*

It's really amazing to me that most of us would rather believe in a lie than accept the truth. Most of the time, we unconsciously choose to trust our fear rather than God, forming habits destructive to our spiritual journey.

For example, throughout our lives, we worry about many things, making ourselves totally miserable in the process. How many of the things we worry about really come true? Ten percent? Five percent? More likely than not, the percentage is very tiny! Yet, in spite of personal experience, we continue to believe in the fear that continues to lie to us all the time.

Yet, when God speaks to us and calls us to do good, most of us choose the other way and run because of our fears and unbelief. We make all kinds of excuses like, "How do I know it's God?" The only way you will ever find out is to just do it!

WHY WE TRUST FEAR INSTEAD OF GOD

We have no problem trusting fear because we have, in a sense, spent a lifetime sleeping with the enemy. We are so comfortable with the enemy of fear that we mistake him for a friend. We have grown so comfortable living with our fears that we find it difficult to release them.

We also have a problem with trusting God because we have not spent enough time with Him to find out if He is trustworthy.

Faith is developed over time by trusting God and seeing the results of obeying Him. Faith breeds faith, and obedience leads to more obedience as we learn God's truth.

This is how God explained it to me in my spiritual journal:

"*It takes faith to see My faithfulness.*

"*When you give Me your heart, I will give you the desires of your heart.*

"*When you place Me first, I will answer you first.*

"*When you seek after Me, I will appear before you.*

"*When you follow Me, I will lead you.*

"*When you obey Me, I will fulfill My will through you.*

"*I will never turn My back on you, even if you turn your back on Me, for I am faithful.*

"*It is My unfailing and everlasting love that always conquers and draws you back to Me.*

"*Therefore, learn to love like I love you.*"

How God Really Healed Our Marriage

Now, let me show how this works in real life. Remember I told you that when God spoke to me the first time He gave me marriage counseling—after all the psychologists and psychiatrists had failed. He told me the same line. "*Love your wife, Tere, unconditionally as I have loved you.*"

I acted on this instruction immediately, and I apologized to my wife and asked for her forgiveness.

That was a good-faith effort of repentance. Repentance is when we know we have gone in the wrong direction and turn around after God shows us the truth. If I had not listened to God and still continued in my old ways, my second marriage would have surely ended in another divorce.

My apology was just the first step. Talk is cheap; it's action that counts. As the saying goes, "Don't snow me, show me!" Over the years, God healed our marriage as He taught me to love unconditionally. He has taught me not to attach my life to things but to depend on Him. *The things we hold onto anchor and weigh us down. Whatever we desire ends up owning us.*

God tested me by asking me to give and keep on giving progressively. *Giving is the answer to forgiving, and forgiveness is true love in action.*

First, He asked me to give fifteen thousand dollars to my wife so she could pay off a second mortgage on a house she owned under her name. I said, "But, God, that house is hers, and it will go to her sons. She has a job. Why can't she pay for it?"

"*Just do it!*" He said.

The next thing was writing over the title of the Mercedes to my wife. I said, "But, God, I have already given her the car. Why do I have to change the title, too?"

"*Just do it!*" He said.

Next was the title to the house. I said, "But, God, it's so unfair. She is not writing my name into her house!"

"*Just do it!*" He said.

By the time it came around to the big one—the cancellation of the prenuptial agreement—I knew the answer before God said anything.

I said, "Just do it! Right?"

At every point, I always ended up with a step deeper into obedience. Fights with my wife always drove me to my knees in prayer. Remember? God said, "*I have sent Tere to purify you. Through her, you will learn love and forgiveness. If you love and forgive, you shall have peace.*"

Finally, I was so trained that I voluntarily created a trust so that even after my death, my wife would be taken care of. And now we have peace. We never fight anymore. There is nothing to fight about because we are learning to give of ourselves to each other. Today, we love each other with a much deeper and more meaningful love.

There is only one kind of love in God's eyes: unconditional love. Anything else is a substitute.

FAITH COMES WHEN WE OBEY AND ACT

Faith comes from a word from God and is empowered by an action. Power comes when we obey and act on His word. Then we see the results of His truth. I was so impatient that I wanted God to wave His "magic wand" and give me instant faith and perfect obedience right away. Faith, however, starts like a seed. When we plant, water, and fertilize it, something miraculous begins to happen. It grows and reproduces after itself. In time, before you know it, you have an entire field.

Let me give you another example. I was raised in Hong Kong, in a culture that respects hard work and self-reliance. If you were a beggar, Hong Kong would not be the ideal city for you to ply your trade. Charitable giving is not on the list of most people's priorities.

The time came when a new governor came into office, nine months later, and I was relieved of my position as CEO of Maryland Public Television—without cause. It is a very long story of power, politics, and betrayal.

My faith had become part of the problem because it was not "politically correct." I felt compelled to defend my religious freedom, so I engaged a major law firm in Washington, D.C. to represent me.

So here I was, fired for the first time in my life with no reason given and no severance package. I was devastated! I had no income. I felt dead poor. (And I had thousands of dollars in legal fees to pay.) I thought I had no future, either. Do you see how our fears deceive us?

Day after day, I was a prisoner in my own home. On one bitterly cold winter day, with the house buried under four feet of snow, I turned on the water and nothing came out. I flushed the toilet and nothing moved. When the plumber finally came to fix the problem, it was the well. The bill came to $1,003.00. It was a surprise bill that I dreaded.

Not long after that, I opened the mail and knew that I had received my miracle. My sister sent me $1000 out of the blue and for no particular reason. She has never sent me money like that before. I was high as a kite!

THE TEST: SOWING THE THOUSAND-DOLLAR MIRACLE

While I was at church, a man next to me confided that he had lost his job for the third time. On top of that, his wife had kicked him out of the house. He sent an alarm signal, saying, "I am losing my faith. I can't take it anymore."

I was minding my own business and praising God for my little miracle when a voice suddenly said, "*I want you to give that man the thousand dollars.*"

I paused and thought, *How do I know that's God talking? Let me pray about this to be sure.*

Then I thought, *It couldn't be my selfish self that would tempt me to do such a selfless thing.*

So I asked God, "Why did You give me the thousand dollars, only to take it away again? That's very disappointing."

He replied, "*I blessed you so you could learn to be a blessing. I gave you a miracle so you could learn how to be a miracle.*"

At the time, it was just too profound for me to understand. I even felt like I was being tricked into something. (That's why I keep a spiritual journal.)

But, I knew in my heart that it was God, and I trusted Him. So I knew the answer…just do it!

I slipped a thousand-dollar check in the offering envelope and wrote, "God loves you. He heard your prayers and is giving this to you." I gave it to the man instead of to the usher.

Back then, I only gave between ten and twenty dollars when the ushers came around. Even though I had absolutely no income at the time, I still gave regularly. But one thousand dollars was unthinkable!

When I obeyed God, miracles started. This story illustrates some timeless spiritual truths: "If you sow, you reap. What you sow is what you reap. The more you sow, the more you reap."[3]

Days passed by, and then the doorbell rang. When you have been unemployed for a while, even the ring of a doorbell can be the highlight of your day. But this doorbell was not the miracle I was looking for.

It was the people from my network. They had come to drop off a stack of boxes. You see, I was not allowed back on the premises to collect my personal belongings because we were in litigation. They stood there and asked for my credit cards, the company car, the television, and all the other hi-tech gadgets that had come along with the job.

This was the most humiliating experience in my life, especially when I had led the network to national prominence and left them with a five million dollar surplus in the bank.

My wife started to cry. Tears streamed down her face. We hadn't bought a car or a television in years; they always came with the job. Now when we had no income, we had to deal with these extra expenditures. Besides that, there was still that stack of bills from the attorney waiting to be paid. Right as the people from the network left, at that very moment, the phone rang. Would you believe it was the man I gave the thousand dollars to?

He said, "I found a job! I am working at a used car place, but I hate it. There is only one good thing. Every night I can take home any car I want from the lot. If you ever need a car, you can borrow my Honda. It's in great shape. I also have a forty-five-inch, state-of-the-art TV that I don't have enough room for."

I hung up the phone in total amazement. I asked my wife, "How does he know?"

Tere said, "It must be God comforting us." God is faithful. He knows what we need even before we ask.[4]

REAPING A MIRACLE HARVEST

Shortly after that, the miracle harvest began. First, consulting assignments started to trickle in. Then the chairman changed the termination to a resignation and offered me a financial settlement. The full board gave me a glowing letter of recommendation for my nine years of service.

Before long, job offers started to come in, and God launched me into an entirely new career serving the poor and needy that surpassed my wildest dreams.

After that experience, I decided to never run away from God when He "tempts" me to do good. I learned to just do it! As the years went by, it became easier and easier to obey God, to just let go whether it was money, power, control, things, or time.

As I followed God step by step, that thousand-dollar miracle multiplied itself over and over again. For example, this past year, we were able to give six times my annual income from the early years to help others. That's the miracle of obedience, which leads to our ultimate blessing.

It is possible because God is the original giver. No one can outgive God, for He said, "Give, and it will be given back to you, multiplied!"[5]

God blesses us so we can be a blessing; He gives us miracles so we can be a miracle for Him.

Obey God the next time He asks you to do good. Trust in His goodness instead of your fears. Try it, and experience a miracle in your life.

Now stop doubting and just do it!

Endnotes

1. See Romans 12:3.
2. See Hebrews 11:6.
3. See Galatians 6:7-9.
4. See Matthew 6:8.
5. See Mark 4:24.

CONCLUSION

Let us then labour for an inward stillness-
An inward stillness and an inward healing
That perfect silence where the lips and heart
Are still, and we no longer entertain
But God alone speaks in us, and we wait
In singleness of heart, that we may know
His will, and in the silence of our spirits
That we may do His will, and do that only.

(Longfellow)

Revelations are God's invitations to change;

obstacles are the stepping stones to change.

What we are is God's gift to us;

what we become is our gift to God.

Jesus Christ is the ultimate revelation of God's love
to man;

when we love, we become God's ultimate testimony to the world.

(An excerpt from my spiritual journal)

Revelations Are God's Invitations to Change

When we hear from God, we receive revelations of His truth. Everything is laid bare. Everything is revealed. We see the truth, the whole truth, and nothing but the truth. The blinders on our eyes are lifted, the planks are removed, our rose-colored glasses disappear. Everything looks clear!

Revelations are God's invitations to change. Obstacles are the stepping stones to change. Change is a sign that we are alive.

If we are living, we are constantly growing and changing. Although everything in this physical world tends to disintegrate with the passage of time, our spirits can be perfected with time.

There is nothing we can do to reverse the natural physical laws of aging and of the deterioration of the mind and the body. The best we can do is slow down the aging process through healthier diets, exercise, and new wonder drugs. But, our spirits have the potential of continuous growth without limitation (because they are eternal), thus developing a better life for ourselves and for others.

We are spirits temporarily traveling in our bodies, having experiences during this short journey called life. The character of our spirits shines through no matter what we do to hide it; who we are radiates wherever we are, whatever we do, and whenever we speak. And who we are is the result of the collective accumulation of all the choices we have made over time.

What Kind of Spirit Do You Have?

Some people have a critical and judgmental spirit while others have a sweet and loving spirit. Some are arrogant and prideful while others are humble and gentle. Some are impatient and worried while others are peaceful and confident. You can sense a person's presence by his or her spirit almost immediately when that person enters a room.

What kind of presence do you have? What kind of spirit do you project? I am not talking about something we are born with; this is something we develop through the choices we make over our lifetimes. We can't do anything about the past, but we can change our futures. We can change our presence and our lives. I am an example of what hearing God can do to change the very heart and spirit of a person.

If we want to change our presence, we must change our spirits. Change starts in the inward man. If we want to change our spirits, we must change our thinking. Our thoughts are the seeds that give birth to our words and actions, which in turn materialize into our character over time.

We have the free will to choose. We can choose to hear God and obey His divine invitation to love, or we can choose to close our ears and reject His communication. We can obey His direction and do unto others as we would have them do unto us, or we can disobey and do unto others what we don't want done unto ourselves.

When we accept God's invitation to love, we step into a dimension of divine opportunity for personal growth. Sometimes this experience seems more like a stumbling block to self, but in the end it always turns out to be a stepping stone to further spiritual development.

God is love. God wants what is best for us. His love is not dictatorial; He gives us freedom to choose.

Mankind is the highest form of created life, created in His image. He gave us the freedom to make choices. But, with freedom come risk, responsibility, and accountability.

The choices and decisions you make accumulate in your spirit. What have you stored up in the treasure chest of your heart in thoughts, feelings, and emotions that have been affected by those choices?

What Kind of Presence Do You Project?

Do you worry and have excessive anxieties over something that may never occur?

Do you experience undue stress and strain over situations that you cannot control?

Do you have unwarranted fears and uneasiness over the possibility of failure or loss?

Do you carry the heavy burden of broken relationships?

Do you regularly fear the threat of sickness and disease?

Do you constantly dread the prospect of unemployment or financial reversal?

Do you have confusion, chaos, and crisis in your life?

You are the cause and not the effect; you are the master and not the victim. Remember, whatever you are willing to put up with in your life is exactly what you are going to get. If you sleep with the enemy long enough, you will cease to control your life. His control is projected as that of a faithful friend when, in reality, he is a ruthless tyrant. God comes to break that control through change in your inner spiritual life.

Do You Want to Change?

Do you need clarity and enlightenment regarding the choices and decisions facing you?

Do you need meaning and purpose in your work and daily life?

Do you desire passion and direction for your life?

If you want to change and you don't know how, it doesn't help to keep asking yourself how you can change. In fact, your erroneous thinking is what created the problem in the first place. So wouldn't it make sense to ask the One who created you?

Of course, you can begin by seeking truth that is already revealed. Study the Scriptures and learn from the spiritual experiences of those in biblical times. Find friends who have already made spiritual progress on their journey. God will not reveal more truth to you until you decide to walk in the truth He has already given you.

Ultimately, you alone must discover what you know of truth through personal experience. Only you can experience the reality of God through responding to the pull of His grace and by the push of constant seeking.

Don't be satisfied with other people's versions of truth; they are only partial truths.

Don't be content with their hand-me-down, secondhand revelations.

Don't be gratified by hearing about other people's experiences of God.

Don't be impressed with their miracles.

God made *you* to be a miracle.

SEEK TO HEAR GOD YOURSELF

If you really want to know how to hear God, you will have to seek Him yourself. Again, it takes a serious commitment of time and effort to develop any meaningful relationship, including one with God. Ultimately, your ability to hear God will depend on the quality of your relationship with Him. Love and trust can be developed only with the passage of time. Only through experience will you be able to truly discern and trust the voice of God. (Keeping a spiritual journal will help you keep score.)

In my early walk with God, I was so anxious to ask Him for help with my problems that on many occasions I projected my needs and desires onto my hearing. That led to great disappointments.

We have a tendency to hear what we want to hear and see what we want to see. That is why I want to share with you what I have learned, so that you can avoid the same mistakes.

HOW DO I KNOW IF I AM HEARING GOD?

First, God is spirit and He is eternal.[1] His perspective is always bigger than ours. He focuses more on the eternal than the temporal. *When God talks, He unveils spiritual principles that help correct our erroneous thinking. God is always more interested in who we are than what we do. What we do flows out of who we are. So God starts with changing who we are.*

I remember the time when I asked God a specific question about whether I should sell a particular mutual fund that day. He replied, *"Make money your slave, or money will make you its slave."* Then He proceeded to teach me how to avoid the powerful attraction of money. Then He taught me that giving to help those who are in need is the answer. Giving to others breaks the power of greed inside us. Truly, His ways are not our ways.

God's voice is loving because He is a God of love. He will not condemn us with the voice of a judgmental parent. Rather, He gently helps us see the errors in our ways, lovingly convicts us of our wrong actions, and brings us to repentance by the power of His goodness and patience. God's direction in our lives will always teach us to turn our focus away from ourselves and onto others. He teaches us how to reach out to others in loving-kindness. At the center of love is giving, and the heart of giving requires sacrifices. These sacrifices build the nature of God in us.

What God tells us to do is seldom what our ego and our flesh want to do. Honestly, who wants to give away their hard-earned money or their time? That's our life! But when God showed me that the only way to have a more abundant life is by giving it away, like God did with Jesus, then I wised up. This was the beginning of my course in divine wisdom.

Jesus Christ is the ultimate revelation of God's love to man. God revealed, testified, and demonstrated His unconditional love through the sacrifice of Himself...in His only Son. When we accept God's gift of Jesus Christ, turn from our sinful ways, and learn to love like Him, we become God's gift to mankind. When we love like Jesus, we become God's ultimate testimony to the world.

When you seek and hear God, the Master Teacher Himself will reveal to you the secrets of the Kingdom that remain hidden from most people. He will shed light on the truth, and you will say, "Once I was blind, but now I see!" Your ability to see spiritual realities will continue to grow.

When you think you have heard from God but are not sure, learn to wait on Him and He will confirm His word in many ways. Being in the Scriptures will strengthen your hearing ability. God will not contradict what He has already revealed as truth; He is a God of clarity.

If you are facing an important decision, ask God for multiple confirmations, including circumstances. You also should consult with wise and godly people whom you trust. Together, these will give you a sense of "knowing" that God really spoke to you.

I can assure you of this: If you heard God speak, you will experience a deep sense of peace and calm that is beyond understanding. You will feel this peace independent of whatever outward circumstances you are facing.

Ultimately, enlightenment finds its ultimate reality in the actions we take and the lives we live, not simply in the words we speak.

When you hear God, the focus of your life will change. You will stop focusing on the material and start seeking the spiritual. You will stop praying for blessings and start becoming a blessing. You will stop chasing after miracles and start being a miracle. You have discovered God's divine paradoxes.

A Life of Abundance and Significance

The Scriptures say, "The fruit of the Spirit is love, joy, peace, patience, kindness, goodness, faithfulness, gentleness and self-control...."[2]

When you listen to God's Holy Spirit and obey His instructions, you will begin your miracle journey of faith. God will continue to transform your heart and change your spirit. He will awaken the spirit in you. He will develop the real you. He will teach you how to love and serve others and to live a life of abundance and significance.

When you hear God, you receive from the ultimate source of divine wisdom. That wisdom will penetrate your defenses and break through your denials. It will clarify your vision and wipe out your illusions. It will help you overcome all your human weaknesses that stunt your growth as a child of God.

Then you can develop love for those who are not lovable. You can have joy during the storms of your personal trials. You can experience peace in the midst of conflict. You can learn patience in the furnace of affliction. You can show kindness to those who are unkind. You can display goodness toward those who hurt you. You can demonstrate faithfulness to those who are unfaithful. You can show gentleness to those who are harsh.

You can exhibit self-control when there is justification for revenge.

Then you will know why hearing God is the ultimate blessing!

Endnotes

1. See John 4:24.
2. Galatians 5:22-23.

Additional copies of this book and other
book titles from DESTINY IMAGE are
available at your local bookstore.

For a complete list of our titles,
visit us at www.destinyimage.com
Send a request for a catalog to:

Destiny Image® Publishers, Inc.
P.O. Box 310
Shippensburg, PA 17257-0310

*"Speaking to the Purposes of God for This
Generation and for the Generations to Come"*